SOJOURN

LEARNING LIFE FROM WILD PLACES

W. VANCE GRACE

WESTBOW
PRESS
A DIVISION OF THOMAS NELSON

WestBow Press books may be ordered through booksellers or by contacting:

WestBow Press
A Division of Thomas Nelson
1663 Liberty Drive
Bloomington, IN 47403
www.westbowpress.com
1-(866) 928-1240

ISBN: 978-1-4497-9363-0 (sc)
ISBN: 978-1-4497-9365-4 (hc)
ISBN: 978-1-4497-9364-7 (e)

Library of Congress Control Number: 2013907726

Printed in the United States of America.

WestBow Press rev. date: 04/26/2013

TABLE OF CONTENTS

Acknowledgments ix

Introduction. 1

Sojourning as a Way of Living 23

Chapter 1   Complexity 33

Chapter 2   Weight 61

Chapter 3   Fear 85

Chapter 4   Integration 107

Conclusion 141

Bibliography. 151

About the Author 157

ACKNOWLEDGMENTS

As we journey through life our path is inevitably shared, shaped and travelled with others. While the story of such interaction would read more like a biography which would take a lifetime to flesh out and read, I would be amiss if I did not at least acknowledge some of the people who have shaped my road and with whom I have shared some of the journey.

Zac Noble figures prominently in the pages that follow. We have shared countless miles of road and trail as well as sleepless and often brutal nights in the backcountry together, both in the high mountains and the sprawling deserts. I could not have asked for a travelling companion better suited to my own temperament, skills and inclinations. He has become more than a brother to me over the past fifteen years. Other individuals worth mentioning who have in sharing the trail shared life with me in significant ways include Dave Roepke, Rob McConnell and Brian Baird.

Another group of individuals have been travelling companions in more of a spiritual than physical sense. Doug Grogan has served as my "dad" for almost twenty years. Bill Janas walked with me through some important developing years and in difficult circumstances and never showed me anything less than unconditional love. Bob Hudson, whom I count as a mentor, friend and brother, was instrumental in this piece coming to fruition and in my life being restored.

Most of all, I have had the privilege of sharing this journey in all of its hills, curves, bumps and blind corners with the most amazing woman in the world. Colleen has more than stuck by me now for over two decades. Our three children, Cheyenne, William and Sheridan, have not only watched their dad in his sojourn but have had to endure a sometimes wild and unpredictable ride—which they have done with valor. I wouldn't be who I am without their presence on the journey.

INTRODUCTION

Follow humbly wherever and to whatever abyss
nature leads, or you shall learn nothing.
—THOMAS HENRY HUXLEY

WHEN RANDY MORGENSON disappeared in California's
Sierra Nevada Mountains in 1996, there was nearly immediate
conjecture about how intentional his disappearance may have
been. Morgenson was a veteran backcountry ranger serving in
Sequoia and Kings Canyon National Parks for twenty-eight
summer seasons, and he had gained a reputation for intuitively
knowing how to locate lost hikers simply by piecing together
predictable patterns of human movement with topographic
terrain features. To fellow rangers, it seemed highly unlikely
that Morgenson would have accidentally gotten himself into
a situation that he would not have been able to escape. The
questions regarding Morgenson's failure to make scheduled radio
contact in July of 1996 swirled around his apparent frustration
and depression, both of which were apparent when he had

returned for the season earlier in the year. Many were familiar with the marriage issues Morgenson and his wife had these days, and Morgenson had voiced some uncharacteristic musings about the validity of his years of work in the backcountry during discussions with his supervisor. At the very least, those who knew Morgenson believed that something was wrong and that it was possible that Randy had purposefully decided to get lose in the wild.

Jon Krakauer popularized the story of Christopher McCandless in his 1996 book *Into the Wild*. In 1990, McCandless had left behind a recent degree from Emory University, a substantial savings account, and his well-to-do New England family to disappear into the wild places of western America. His body was found two years later in the Alaskan interior. McCandless was a brilliant young man who was steeped in literature and philosophy, and he eventually found himself questioning the validity of many cultural values like consumption and at least initially, romantic love and relationships. For two years, McCandless wandered the western states mostly alone, though he interacted enough with other people that Krakauer could get a fairly accurate picture of this man's personality and his reasoning for tramping about as he did. The picture that emerges is one of a successful man frustrated with life as it had been conceived for him, a man determined to find some answers by disappearing alone into wild places.

Stories like those of Morgenson and McCandless become popular reads because they seem to be precisely what so many of us in our modern context could see ourselves resorting to, especially those of us who are trying to figure out how to "practice life" despite being frustrated with some of our socially constructed realities (i.e., how to deal with the onset of a midlife depression and emptiness). Increasing numbers of young and middle-aged men have longed for the opportunity to disappear in some form, disillusioned in one way or another with the world they inhabit or the world they have created for themselves through education, work, and consumption. Confusion seems to mount as do bills and responsibilities, and many of us never anticipated life would seem so empty.

How do we really live, especially when it all seems to go wrong or we don't feel as if we know what we're doing in the first place? There have been a number of authors in recent years addressing the ongoing crisis of American life despite our wealth and leisure and the abundance of entertainment options in the twenty-first century. For many, entertainment and other distractions are not as effective as they were once designed to be. Pascal warned us nearly four hundred years ago that entertainment was a mere tonic, a distraction from the more crucial issues of the "how" and "why" of life. It often appears that these distracting options are not speaking loudly enough to silence the growing societal disaffection. Likewise, much had been written recently about the rise of interest in spirituality rather than its waning. Apparently, we haven't figured everything out in terms of our science and technology. Americans continue to spend a disproportionate amount of their personal wealth on this program, that vacation, these books in order to try to gain perspective and meaning to life. In a seminal book on the meaning of the life of a male, Robert Bly wrote in *Iron John: A Book about Men*, "Even though we are highly advanced in matters of atomic physics and computer technology, we are still beginners in the labor of learning how to live. We really don't know what we are doing" (Bly, 2004).

The result is a plethora of frustrated musicians telling us their stories through poetry. Eddie Vedder sings in "Life Wasted," "I've seen this home inside your head / All locked doors and unmade beds / Open sores unattended / Let me say just once that / I have faced it, a life wasted / I am never going back again." The issue may be increasingly pressing in the current and coming years as it feels as if an absence—the absence of challenge and the meaning which would accompany that challenge—is the particular plague on my own generation. Raised in the postwar age of entitlement, we believed that the good life or at least the real life consisted of school, a career, and an increasing climb up the ladder of authority, expertise, and income. We haven't had any great wars or depressions, and therefore, we have had to largely make things up. It is likely that due to years of culture-wide fatherlessness, too few of us were ever initiated into the world of men or meaning. Douglas Coupland's *Life After God* was once the voice of those of us just now on the verge of middle age. "I think there was a trade-off somewhere along the line. I think the price we paid for our golden life was an inability to fully believe in love; instead we gained an irony that scorched everything it touched. And I wonder if this irony is the price we paid for the loss of God" (Coupland, 1994). When we were growing up, many of my friends made a habit of relentlessly mocking those we called "yuppies," individuals we believed were sellouts from the hippie era who once believed in fighting the system and who were now engaged in earning a six-figure income from the very same system. The reality I now recognize is that at least teens of the 60s had something like a cause to engage in while my own generation only had what authors have now come to call societal angst. As a consequence, we don't necessarily know how to engage constructively with what frustrates us, and instead, we only unleash cynicism on everything around us while we lose ourselves in our music. Even for many of my close friends and contemporaries, who, I assumed, had avoided such crises, they find somewhere around forty an insatiable appetite for meaning and understanding.

I realize that every quest is intensely personal and takes on individual forms and a unique series of questions. Each person responds in varying degrees of frustration and desperation to the issues of life. Many people will never feel that life is devoid of meaning or go off the deep end in search of some kind of perspective on what we're doing here in the world or what might bring some kind of meaning to this existence. But I know I had lost all perspective and hope, and I didn't have the abiding sense that life was as it should be. Maybe, just maybe I had cast life in the wrong light and had been listening to the wrong stories. Maybe what I had been told all along about how to make a living—how to make a life, really—wasn't real at all. Maybe I needed a different story. Maybe my own crisis was the result of failing to listen to some things I already knew and a failure to listen to what I was really learning. A lot of this comes down to disappointed expectations. What happens when we expect certain reactions to our actions that never find their way to fruition? If I did this or if I do that or change these things, shouldn't I expect meaning, perspective, joy, and an abiding peace? Not that we necessarily need to feel good all the time, but isn't there some kind of sense out there of *shalom*, the sense that things are as they should be?

Maybe we need a new metaphor, a metaphor that can embrace the complexity of life and take into consideration weight, our fear, and the need for integration—something that can provide perspective on life that isn't steeped in empty promises, something so recent in the experience of the human condition that its sustainability and power to construct meaningful life are still highly suspect. Our current levels of leisure, wealth, and purported "comfort" exist for more people at levels never before known, and still, we long for some kind of authentic existence. Perhaps this metaphor is not really a new metaphor at all but rather a very ancient one that defined life even in this country up until the early 1900s. It may be that the absence of this defining factor for too many modern Americans (only decades after its absence) has led us to the fallout we are currently experiencing. I believe that the metaphor that can help us figure out life is the wilderness: the wild places of the desert, the mountain, and the jungle, namely those places which at one time and for the majority of human existence constituted the context out of which people lived and defined life. Speaking specifically of male initiation but revealing larger truths, Robert Bly states, "To receive initiation truly means to expand sideways into the glory of oaks, mountains, glaciers, horses, lions, grasses, waterfalls, deer. We need wilderness and extravagance. Whatever shuts a human being away from the waterfall and the tiger will kill him" (Bly, 2004).

In *Wilderness and the American Mind*, Roderick Nash chronicles the place for the idea and metaphor of wilderness in the development of America as a philosophical, theological, and aesthetic idea. Nash tracks the transition of thinking about wild places from the theology of early settlers which convinced them that wilderness was the haunt of evil spirits that would need to be pushed back and subdued by God's gift of the civilizing presence of humans. His work precedes from there to the movement in the latter half of the twentieth century to preserve wilderness as a necessary and important aspect of what it means to be human. Henry David Thoreau was a seminal thinker in this regard: "'The forest and wilderness furnish the tonics and barks which brace mankind.' Thoreau grounded his argument on the idea that wildness was the source of vigor, inspiration, and strength. It was, in fact, the essential 'raw-material of life.' Human greatness of any kind depended on tapping this primordial vitality. Thoreau believed that to the extent a culture, or an individual, lost contact with wildness it became weak and dull. 'In short, all good things are wild and free'" (Nash, 1967).

Wilderness can be seen as a metaphor, as something to lay over the top of life for some kind of perspective on what is happening to us and why. Having emerged from the Age of Entitlement without adequate lessons on who we are or what life would look like, we stand in need of something to frame our experience. Wild places provide a way to understand the components of life and learn some of the lessons we likely missed in our race through school and the ascendency of our careers. Wilderness has served as both a place and an idea that (at least in my own journey) has provided the only sense I could make of my existence. I have been visiting wild places for years—as a youth growing up in Wyoming, as a student visiting the wilds of northern Minnesota, and as a resident of Colorado making frequent trips to mountains, deserts, and mesas. What I didn't recognize until recent days, however, was why these settings have always been so crucial to the way I live life. The bottom recently fell out of my life, and I found myself having to put some pieces back together with the help of a counselor who helped me recognize that it has always been the wilderness where I really lived an integrated life. This was especially true during those times when nothing else around me seemed to make any sense, and I found myself lacking any coherent sense of self-identity. Metaphor has always been important for us. Jesus taught—and obscured—many things through the use of story and metaphor. Enduring truths have come to us through metaphor. Stories like *The Lord of the Rings Trilogy* are so compelling and timeless partially because they serve as a metaphor of greater truths. C. S. Lewis, whom we'll have opportunity to walk with later, was a master of utilizing metaphor as something to lay over life in order to teach us something important, especially through *The Chronicles of Narnia* and *The Space Trilogy*.

Joseph Conrad utilizes this very organizing idea of wilderness as a metaphor in his classic *Heart of Darkness*. When this short novel was written in 1899, the Western world was still very much in the throes of the development of the industrial and scientific revolutions. Conrad questions what humanity stands to lose in a culture arrogant and fat with its own accomplishments but also apparently removed from any real self-knowledge. The book's protagonist, Marlow, is a steamer captain hired to pilot a small vessel up river into the thick African interior in order to discover the fate of the station manager of a remote outpost. As he progresses upriver, Marlow continuously reflects on the role of the wilderness he is moving through, particularly as it relates to a Western European context, quickly removing all traces or threats of the presence of anything not yet brought under the sway of "civilization."

Existing in a pristine and primitive condition, wild places for Conrad hold important and crucial self-knowledge that modern life has hidden or forgotten about. The haunt of wild beasts,

SOJOURN

wild and uncultivated men, and forests, the wilderness holds an ancient wisdom about our souls that has become obscured by our pedestrian lives. The revelation of such wisdom, however, can at times seem rather frightening because we sometimes don't know what we should do with actual passion and a life with primal urges as opposed to the life that is immersed always in the man-made and engineered, the life that is closely guarded and highly controlled. At one point, Marlow and his crew encounter wild natives, inhabitants of a wild land: "Unexpected, wild and violent as they had been, they had given me an irresistible impression of sorrow. The glimpse of the steamboat had for some reason filled those savages with unrestrained grief. The danger, if any, I expounded, was from our proximity to a great human passion let loose" (Conrad, 1910). The grief came from the advance of what we think of as "civilization" into wild places and with it, a reduction in the ability to know ourselves and the great human passions. It is only in the wilderness, far from the dwellings and creations of a modern culture, that any self-knowledge is possible. Conrad warned, however, that we are not likely to be comfortable with self-knowledge because at this point in history, such will seem primitive and full of a passion that's unusual for Western, civilized men and women.

> You can't understand, how could you? With
> solid pavement under your feet, surrounded by
> kind neighbors ready to cheer you or fall on
> you, stepping delicately between the butcher
> and the policeman, in the holy terror of scandal
> and gallows and lunatic asylums—how can you
> imagine what particular region of the first ages
> a man's untrammeled feet may take him into
> by the way of solitude—utter solitude without

9

a policeman—by way of silence—utter silence, where no warning voice of a kind neighbor can be heard whispering of public opinion? Those little things make all the great difference. When they are gone you must fall back on your own innate strength, upon your own capacity for faithfulness. (Conrad, 1910)

Following my own prolonged crisis and personal darkness, I finally realized that my own passion for wild places stems from the fact that wilderness has always served as a metaphor laying over the rest of life, teaching me and providing the context to integrate and find a sense of shalom. As I sought to extract the lessons for life, I recognized that apart from my trips to the wilderness, whether in success or defeat, I had little means of understanding the ebb and flow of life and how to deal with the people, places, and circumstances in my midst. It was these trips that taught me about the fundamental elements of life—complexity, weight, and fear—and how to respond to these things in a way that might make life livable. These are the elements of life that I now believe ancient cultures intuited and lived and thrived through—elements we have sought to engineer and program out of life, much to our detriment. We are witnessing the current crisis for many of my generation to figure out the why and wherefore of life because we don't know what to do with the naturalness of complexity, weightiness, or fear. I feel much like Everett Ruess, a young man in his early twenties who disappeared into the Utah desert after he lived for years wandering around the wild places of the west. "I had some terrific experiences in the wilderness since I wrote you last—overpowering, overwhelming. But then I am always being overwhelmed. I require it to sustain life" (Rusho, 2002).

SOJOURN

This isn't intended as an answer book, as if at forty-one years old, I have figured it all out. But life and wild places have provided me with a perspective out of which I am learning to look at and appreciate the multiplicity inherent in life. I realize that earning a life of substance takes many more years than I have yet lived and fear will likely always be present in some form. But that's precisely why I am endeavoring to write about sojourning. We must see healthy life as a journey if we're ever going to be willing to leave the self-created and often illusory safety of the home ground we have formed around ourselves. It is the process and how we journey that determines if we can get through life as integrated, whole, and healthy individuals. Approaching life as a journey, however hard it may be at times, and learning from that process can provide an important corrective for lives otherwise stuck in the unreal. The alternative is to perpetually lack crucial self-knowledge. A picture of a person who possessed a certain respectability and yet who didn't know themselves is provided in the protagonist of Joseph Conrad's *Lord Jim*.

> His prospects were good. He was gentlemanly, steady, tractable, with a thorough knowledge of his duties; and in time, when yet very young, he became chief mate of a fine ship, without ever having been tested by those events of the sea that show in the light of day the inner worth of a man, the edge of his temper, and the fibre of his stuff; that reveal the quality of his resistance and the secret truth of his pretenses, not only to others but also to himself. (Conrad, 1899)

Wallace Stegner, one of the great fiction and nonfiction writers of the wild places and lessons of Western wildernesses, wrote,

"The west being what it is, a westerner trying to examine his life has trouble finding himself in any formed or coherent society. His confrontations are therefore likely to be with landscape, which seems to define the west and its meaning better than any of its forming cultures, and with himself in the context of that landscape" (Stegner, 1985). Stegner's original point had to do with the West as a young region geographically without the ties to the received European culture, which Eastern states tended to gravitate toward. The lesson may be extended in our contemporary context, however, because of the dearth of a sense of any "formed or coherent society." For a generation bereft of great crises, wars, or fathers, it may be that looking to the wilderness of a desert or mountain landscape can provide a much-needed context from which to derive meaning.

While I was growing up in southwest Wyoming, my father was a land surveyor. He spent a great deal of time wandering through desert regions, sagebrush flats, and mountainous terrain where there was often little more than a small trail for a road. His work often required him to hike into roadless areas in order to survey and stake out what would be the initial road into a remote canyon. When my brother and I were out of school, we would often have the privilege of going to work with him to offer what help we could—but I think more often we simply wanted to give my mother a break from the antics of small boys as we found wide open spaces to burn off plenty of energy. I remember countless hours spent kicking through the sagebrush of wide-open country, searching for small brass corner markers about the diameter of a doorknob often buried under layers of sand. It was difficult discovery work in the days before widespread GPS use. Becoming quickly bored with such needle-in-the-haystack work, my brother any I would turn to the livelier pursuits of hunting blue-bellied lizards, horned frogs, and scorpions. These summers served as my introduction to the wild, uninhabited country of southwest Wyoming, and I had no idea how deeply the love of the desert and sky and space was working its way into my heart and concept of self. I hadn't been away from home long as an adult before I found myself longing for the solitude and silence of such wide spaces. This is the context from which I emerged and soon returned to as a means of understanding the lessons necessary to make a life.

Wallace Stegner provides another metaphor in his fictional work *Angle of Repose*. The heroine of the story is the narrator's grandmother, who happened to be a cultured artist raised in privilege on the East Coast in the late 1800s. When Susan found herself married to a mining engineer, a thoroughgoing Westerner, she has to reexamine the point of life separated from all she had based reality on. Susan found her life adrift and in upheaval living in the absence of any formed or coherent culture. The story is about this loss and the process of trying to discover what life might look like firmly set in the varying landscapes of the unsettled West. The title of the novel is drawn from the angle at which rocks and dirt calvings from a hillside finally come to rest. Stegner narrates,

> Remember the one who wanted to know where you learned to handle so casually a technical term like "angle of repose? ... you were too alert to the figurative possibilities of words not to see the phrase as descriptive of human as well as detrital rest. As you said, it was too good for mere dirt. You tried to apply it to your own wandering and uneasy life ... There was a

time when everything was wrong … Did you come down out of that into some restful 30 degree angle and life happily ever after? Was the quiet I always felt in you really repose? … If Henry Adams could make a theory of history by applying the second law of thermodynamics to human affairs, I ought to be entitled to base one on the angle of repose, and may yet. (Stegner, 1971)

So the metaphor goes. Many men my own age seem to be tumbling down the hillside. Without being very well equipped with the skills necessary to really make a life of shalom, we know little else than a wandering and uneasy life. We seemed to have missed the significant ties to any formed or coherent society. Indeed, the metaphor of an angle of repose is too good for mere dirt. We return to landscape—to wild and uninhabited places—as a means to find life. Our confrontation can be in wilderness because it naturally demonstrates realities that we live and swim in daily but can't seem to get a handle on any other way. I believe that we want and need some repose from the uneasy and wandering life, and I believe that we can find it in the lessons of the hills.

I want to explore and make explicit some of these lessons from my own time in the hills and what reflection on these trips has taught me about life. I believe that if we learn to expect something different from life, we might be able to find our way and place in it. When we *expect* order, freedom from weight, and fear and find life in its actuality butting up against these expectations and disappointing them, then too many of us seem to enter prolonged periods of personal darkness and depression.

We may lash out at that—as I did—or simply quietly resign ourselves to the ongoing discrepancy of life. Either way, I believe we will never find the integration we were meant for and need—never come to an angle of repose—until we learn those things that older cultures simply intuited because of their natural connection to their environments. At the very least, I hope that more people will be motivated to discover the lessons of the wilderness because they are lessons a book can only allude to. They are lessons that need to be experienced in order to be integrated into life. Jack Kerouac said, "No man should go through life without once experiencing healthy, even bored solitude in the wilderness, finding himself depending solely on himself and thereby learning his true and hidden strength."

The alternatives to learning these lessons from life and coming to the angle of repose tend to be dramatic and far-reaching. People can turn forty and believe that they have done it all wrong, that this isn't what life was meant to be and that there must be some other way to thrive and find shalom. Some pack up and walk out on life in this mindset, leaving family and friends behind so that they can chase something else as the means to the answers, and they end up looking more like boulders picking up increasing speed as they tumble down the hillside than they look like objects coming to rest. Others merely ensconce themselves deeper in life as it already is—a higher-paying job, more religion, a more comfortable living space, a nicer vehicle, maybe giving more volunteer time. These individuals may gain the respect of others and avoid the derision of the one who runs wild, but they careen off the slope nonetheless as they quietly die inside. Sigurd Olson described the dangers inherent in such a move toward a life of consumptive comfort when he said, "There is a penalty for too much comfort and ease, a penalty of lassitude and inertia and the frustrated feeling that comes with unreality" (Nash, 1973). Henry David Thoreau was partially famous for quipping that "the mass of men lead lives of quiet desperation."

A life that can interact with wild places is a life forced into intentionality. We are not allowed to simply lounge about in some pretend and self-created comfort. There is a high price to pay for abandoning received principles and lashing out wildly. It may be this generation's only recourse to learn about life, namely what Viktor Frankl and Dietrich Bonheoffer learned in the harsh solitude of prison or what many of our grandparents learned in the scarcity of the depression or the foxholes of WWII. Aldo Leopold was right. "All history consists of successive excursions from a single starting point, to which man returns again and again to organize another excursion for durable values. That starting point is wilderness" (Nash, 1973). It is such durable values I hope to talk about, and indeed, they are drawn from wilderness.

Henry David Thoreau moved to an uninhabited shore of Walden Pond because he was desperate to learn what existence might really mean.

> I went to the woods because I wished to live deliberately, to front only the essential facts of life, and see if I could not learn what it had to teach, and not, when I come to die, discover that I had not lived. I did not wish to live what was not life. … I wanted to live deep and suck all the marrow of life, to live so sturdily and Spartan-like as to put to rout all that was not life, to cut a broad swath and shave close, to

drive life into a corner and reduce it to its lowest terms, and, if it proved to be mean, why then to get the whole and genuine meanness of it. (Thoreau, 1999)

So I want to take wilderness—primarily that of western American deserts and mountains—as a metaphor to lay over our lives so that we might learn something about finding a kind of angle of repose, a sense of shalom. While the lessons will likely keep coming for me as long as I have health and strength to visit wild and uninhabited places, I will limit the exploration into four sections introducing what I feel are significant overarching themes that profoundly inform life as it is really confronted. These are perspectives I embrace because of significant time alone in what Belden Lane calls "fierce landscapes." It is indeed in these fierce landscapes that I have found solace. Lane had it right when he said, "There is an unaccountable solace that fierce landscapes offer to the soul" (Lane, 1998).

On Quandry Peak in the Tenmile Range of central Colorado in 2005, I came face-to-face with the complexity of life. Scientists of the emergent school tell us that organisms and organizations that thrive do so in the context of complexity— the razor's edge of optimum health between order and chaos. This is the crucial starting point for the rest of the story. If you are anything like me, then you emerged from college in your early to mid-twenties with a strong sense of order to life. Career, family, accumulation—they were all sought and somewhat controlled by us as a means to discover and live what we had been convinced life consisted of. There was direction and purpose to our movements and decisions, and life was often conceived in terms of black-and-white values.

Everything had its place and reason, and our education had taught us that everything could be engineered and ordered. For many of us on the verge of the significant life changes around forty, however, a grand shift takes place, one that makes our context resemble something more like chaos than order. Our efforts and possessions don't necessarily provide the ends we expected. The order we thought life was lived under gives way to disillusionment and the frustration that not everything simply adds up as we had projected. Both poles—the one of extreme order and the opposite of extreme chaos—are dangerous and unrealistic. Scientists tell us that too much order is stultifying; it leaves little room for movement, adaptation, and flexibility. Everything "in its place" means that nothing can change its place to expand or grow. Chaos is equally detrimental to health because in a chaotic condition, much more is destroyed than created, and a thriving organism or social situation is unlikely to be reached when things are in complete disarray. Wilderness can teach us to walk the healthy line of life as complex—free from stultifying order or unruly chaos.

It was a trip to Gannett Peak through Titcomb Basin in the Wind Rivers of Wyoming that I now reflect back on as the event that gave me significant exposure to the necessary weight of life. This may be one of the more difficult concepts to embrace as many of us may not understand the necessity of living a "weighty" life. A life of weight is one of substance and meaning, but it is often elusive. Moreover, in our contemporary culture, it can be especially difficult to attain this life. In order to add substance or weight to life, we will actually need to move in a direction that can seem quite countercultural, and we will likely have to fight against the tendencies of our inclination toward a light and easy existence. To understand and embrace a life of weight, we need to face hard and uncomfortable things, many of which will require new outlooks on suffering and privation. In a somewhat countercultural move, we may have to unload some of the elements and possessions of life to "lighten up" so that we might move toward lives heavy with significance. Often our comfortable existence, which is insulated by our possessions and conveniences, keeps us moving intellectually and emotionally light through life while we are also fueling our confusion and angst about existence. Too many of us tumble about through the descent of understanding because we have no weight. C. S. Lewis will be informative through his metaphorical language in this regard.

Climbing a glaciated peak in the Indian Peaks Wilderness of Colorado in the fall of 2005, Zac and I both had to face significant fear from our own different perspectives on climbing. It wasn't until more than half a decade later that I understood the important and valuable role fear has to play in our lives—both in healthy and unhealthy ways. We tend to spend a great deal of time and resources attempting to alleviate fear or at least insulate ourselves from experiencing it. There is an interesting dynamic for an individual like myself who actually fears heights to continue to expose him or herself to them on a regular basis, whether in ascending high peaks or rappelling deep into slot canyons in the desert. What took me years to discover was that my courting of fear through frequent exposure to heights was likely due to an unrecognized need to walk toward fear instead of seeking to cover it. Somehow I intuitively knew that a certain amount of fear was good for the soul. I believe that fear, like weight and complexity, is an integral part of the soul's health because its presence serves as a doorway to so many truths about our identities and lives in this world. Acknowledging and walking into the reality of our fear in a deep and honest sense may be the key to finally moving into a life of weighty significance as well as providing the means to our integration. Fear is natural in wild environments when we are taken from our safety and comfort, and it is just as natural for the rest of life as well.

I have had the privilege of visiting the Maze District of Canyonlands National Park on more than one occasion, not only totally alone but the only human inhabitant for hundreds of square miles and the only visitor for a span of months at a time. It is a humbling experience. I visited the desert region of the Maze in February of 2009 and again in 2011 under very different personal circumstances, and hence, I found myself responding very differently to my surroundings. My reflections resemble a kind of before-and-after reaction to this stark and captivating natural wonder. It was here that I believe I began to reflect on the crucial piece of integration necessary for a healthy life. All of us are made up of elements that we accentuate or hide, depending on our backgrounds and circumstances. We may be intellectual, emotional, or physical as a primary means of showing up to our context, often at the expense of the other elements. Psychologists, counselors, and authors far more brilliant than me tell us that a basic need for health is the integration of these elements into our conscious experience as well as expression. Likely the whole point of a book like this is to help us move closer to full and healthy integration so that we might really know what life is meant to be. What I failed to recognize for years was that I was actually attracted to the wilderness because it was the only place where I had ever really been integrated. The work of life is now to allow the metaphor of the outdoors to layer on life wherever it occurs in order to be healthy and whole.

The title of this work, *Sojourn*, is meant to invoke the idea that life is much more like a journey than we often acknowledge. Many are prone to give lip service to the idea of life as a journey without actually internalizing what the idea might entail. For many individuals throughout history, this very idea has been utilized as a truth meant to inform one's whole approach to life. Early followers of Jesus were encouraged to conceive of their lives in terms of a sojourn—a passing-through. They often referred to themselves as aliens, people living in places that were not their homes. Regardless of one's own view of religion, spirituality, and the afterlife, it is apparent that we are at best visitors here. Even if we are privileged to spend eighty years on this earth, we are merely passing through in the form we know life as now. There is a direct correlation to one's trips to the backcountry. We merely pass through at best. This is part of the reason I believe we can learn so much from travels to wild places. We are all travelers, sojourners, and in some important sense, aliens. So like people living in places that are not their homes, there are likely elements of our culture we would do best not to internalize. If indeed life is a journey, then it behooves us to learn to travel well. There are some important lessons we learn from wilderness about our own sojourns, lessons that will likely strike us as counterintuitive if we never journey and only conceive of ourselves as settlers. Before we turn to those lessons, it may be helpful for us to flesh out this idea of life as a sojourn in order to prepare us to travel well.

Sojourning as a Way of Living

In the midst of some of our saner moments, we are likely to reflect on the nature of life as a journey of one kind or another. We understand that we travel through life from birth to death, adding experiences and knowledge of various kinds to the "rucksacks" we travel with. These constitute the things we believe will lead us successfully through our extended trip on spaceship Earth. We all likely intuit the fact that we carry some things throughout life that we would be better off not carrying as well—perhaps some baggage that does little other than slow us down or interfere with our ability to travel well. While the image is probably not a stretch for most of us, the reality of day-to-day life demonstrates a different kind of approach in which traveling well through this existence is the furthest thing from our minds.

In 1973, the songwriter Roger Waters eloquently zeroed in on this issue of life in his song "Time."

Ticking away the moments that make up a dull day / You fritter and waste the hours in an offhand way / Kicking around on a piece of ground in your hometown / Waiting for someone or something to show you the way / Tired of lying in the sunshine staying home to watch the rain / You are young and life is long and there is time to kill today / And then one day you find ten years have got behind you / No one told you when to run, you missed the starting gun.

The word *sojourn* brings to mind the image of an extended journey, usually one with some significance and duration that a mere "trip" doesn't entail. Plato was reported to have said, "It is a common saying, and in everybody's mouth, that life is but a sojourn." The Greek word from the ancient world, as one example, literally means "from the house," and a sojourner is often translated as "alien," referring to someone who lives in a place that is not his or her home. To sojourn then implies an extended journey with some kind of temporary residency in a place not considered one's more permanent home, usually for some purpose or venture that would not be considered a vacation. For such a person, life takes on a form or sense of movement because he or she is somewhat "unsettled" from what is otherwise considered one's settlement or settled state.

The reality is that so many of us spend a great deal of our younger years thinking about little else other than "settling." Many of us, particularly in the Western world, are raised to "settle in" to a family, a career, and/or a home. To live the good life is to fill our garages and family rooms with all of the latest toys and then settle down to enjoy our accumulation—the fruits of our labor.

What if we were to really understand and live as if life were an extended journey? Traveling well in this context required us to carefully examine what we were carrying and what we were leaving behind? I believe that we can learn some important lessons about life from cultures that have conceived of and conducted life on these very terms, not in isolated moments of personal reflection but as defining elements of their entire cultures.

The American Southwest is littered with the remnants of clans, tribes, and groups of people who thrived in one of the most beautiful and harshest environments in the Americas from around 7000 BC until their apparent "disappearance" sometime around 1200. For many of these native peoples, inhabiting the high deserts of the Colorado Plateau, sojourn was basic to their understanding and approach to life. For years known as the Anasazi, these inhabitants of the Four Corners region of the United States left behind the marks of their culture in stone buildings constructed on desert plains or built in protected cliff alcoves and a plethora of artwork panels etched or painted on towering rock walls. Millions of people each year enjoy seeing their story in places like Mesa Verde, Chaco Canyon, Navajo National Monument, and through countless baskets and pottery scattered in museums throughout the West.

In what seems like one of the great mysteries of the ancient world, these tribes and clans mysteriously disappeared from the region they had inhabited for thousands of years and countless generations. In his book on the collapse of various historical societies worldwide, Jared Diamond includes a chapter explaining the dissolution of the Anasazi. In what has become the somewhat standard argument, Diamond attributes the sudden absence of these groups from the regions of the American Southwest, which they had inhabited for centuries, to their own rapacious treatment of the land compounded by a lengthy climate change. As the "Ancient Ones" grew to depend on agriculture as their primary staple, they required more permanent dwellings to care for crops during the growing season. This apparent change in lifestyle allowed for greater population stability and growth while it also contributed to massive deforestation of large regions. Clans would soon be forced to travel hundreds of miles for their timber needs for use in their homes and fires. Desert agriculture also required widespread irrigation, which soon depleted the soil of necessary nutrients to continue to grow the corn and beans for a growing population. Compounding the loss of topsoil through erosion as a result of deforestation and the growing needs of an increasing number of people, archaeologists have identified an unusual prolonged drought occurring sometime in the thirteenth century, one that the people simply could not survive. Massive migrations occurred with the people of an entire region moving to the more fertile and stable environment of the Rio Grande Valley in current-day New Mexico.

Doubtless, many of these conditions actually existed in the Southwest in the 1200s. But author Craig Childs, who has pursued the ancient paths and lifestyles of these people for years, has a different take on their apparent "disappearance" from the areas they inhabited for generations. In his book *House of Rain*, Childs makes the compelling case that such large-scale migrations—sojourns—were as basic an approach to life for this people as was their agricultural practice. Considering the thousands of years of occupation from the earliest Basketmaker periods to the later Pueblo eras, there likely would have been countless drought cycles like the one that was known to have struck the area in the 1200s. Studies demonstrate many periods of mass migration out of a particular area as well as subsequent reinhabitation. There are many indications that the dwelling sites, many of which still survive today, were likely repeatedly inhabited and left only to be renewed by successive generations. It may be that clans and families had known of dwelling sites that would be utilized by ancestors and multiple following generations as natural migration patterns—lengthy patterns covering hundreds of years—very different from the migrations of northern and eastern tribes based simply on the movement of game.

There is also the fascinating dynamic of the importance of roads and travel lines for these ancient people. To this day, there remains visible evidence of ancient and straight roads throughout the Four Corners region. Particularly around the massive structures of Chaco Canyon, ancient highways running starkly across the desert in straight lines for hundreds of miles are still visible from an elevated perspective. Great pains were made to build these roads as straight as possible, often having steps carved into steep sandstone in order to maintain a line of direction as opposed to the modern practice of curving around many obstacles. Comb Wash in southeast Utah and its continuance in Chinle Wash in northeast Arizona was likely another favored north/south travel route because of its relatively consistent trajectory. The efforts of an ancient subsistence culture living in one of the harshest environment on the continent to construct such travel routes is simply another way to reinforce the basic approach to life for a people who saw migration as fundamental to existence. The aesthetic nature of these highways, many of which were often built at greater effort than necessary, demonstrates that they were thought of as more than simple highways for barter and trade.

There is a sense in which the Anasazi understood life as a sojourn. This needs to be distinguished from the more nomadic lifestyle of the tribes of the Great Plains that tended to follow game according to seasons and lived in far more mobile and temporary dwellings. Modern Americans seem to parallel the mentality of the latter group in our own rapid migrations around the country, even considering our semipermanent "houses." We tend to chase an ever-increasing rise in lifestyle in a rather migratory way, feeling that the home we buy this year will likely not be our permanent residence. This does not, however, reflect the Anasazi understanding of life as a sojourn. Agriculture required clans to be in a location for an extended stay, and their stone dwellings demonstrate this stability. At the same time, there was always the sense that this "permanent" place may be only a step along the journey—a sentiment that we might soon return to another place our ancestors had built and perhaps our descendants would follow a road back to this place many generations from now. This was not movement based on the accumulation of wealth as it is for many people today; the journeys of the Anasazi had much more enduring significance.

Childs associates these sojourns with the lifelong journey to the House of Rain. They believed this was the place from which all water emanated—that precious and often rare essential element for life to thrive. Only an agricultural people attempting to survive in the desert can truly appreciate the rain. The patterned travels and migrations were aimed at ultimately finding and dwelling in the House of Rain, and anywhere the clan might settle, regardless for how long, was merely an extended stopover on their way home. The labyrinth of roads was always out there, no matter how settled life appeared, to take them nearer the source of life. Existence was nothing if not an extended journey in the midst of building and growing and raising a family. Though we might practice a semipermanent lifestyle at best in America today, we are not likely to associate our journeys with this focus to move toward a more precious and essential source of life. We are far more like those who chase the plentiful from one field to the next.

This understanding of life is apparent in the messages these people left behind in their artwork etched and painted on the rock walls of canyons throughout the Southwest. One of the most common designs utilized in countless "galleries" consists of a spiraling circle, and it is found virtually everywhere petroglyphs and pictographs occur in any significant number. Although archaeologists are not entirely settled on the precise meanings of any particular design, the spiral has been variously interpreted as signifying migration, life, water—namely the elements that sustain life from birth to death. Certainly migration, movement, life, and the essential elements of life were intimately intertwined for these desert dwellers. One modern tourist brochure from a shop near Flagstaff, Arizona, describes the design like this:

> The Great Seal of the Salt River Pima-Maricopa Indian Community is an ancient pattern. The pattern figured for untold years in Pima baskets

and represents The Maze or House of Se-He-Na. The legend of the 'Man in the Maze' helps children understand the meaning of life. The Maze depicts experiences and choices we make in our journey through life. It illustrates the search for balance—physical, social, mental, and spiritual. In the middle of the maze are found a person's dreams and goals. Legend says when we reach the center, the Sun God is there to greet us, bless us, and pass us to the next world.

While in our postmodern, industrialized society, not many of us in the Western world are so fixated on the basic elements that sustain our physical lives. We nonetheless need and pursue those things that allow life to be fully and naturally lived. Our own migration and pursuit is like that of Chris Cornell who sings, "Nail in my hand, from my Creator / You gave me life, now show me how to live," as we seek to move toward the House of Rain. It is in reality all a journey, an extended migration as life ebbs and flows toward meaning and fulfillment. We would do well to follow the understanding of life modeled for us by these ancient people.

To approach life in these terms and with this understanding would then cause us to consider more carefully what we carry with us as we go on our way. Like any extended journey we might undertake, it is of the utmost importance to take inventory of what we pack as well as what we choose to leave behind. As we move through life, we generally want to equip ourselves so that we are able to travel a clear-cut path, moving as lightly as possible and as free from fear as we can be. In taking this approach, however, it is likely that we are missing critical elements in our outfit. This will become clearer as we move through the section on integration. As we move from our youth to our working years and into middle age, we are generally convinced we cannot travel well with fear, anger, or grief, and hence, we systematically off-load these elements at their first appearance. We will find, however, that integration is virtually impossible without acknowledging these pieces in our lives. It is counterintuitive to leave these things in our pack, though crucial for the journey.

On the other hand, many of us tend to pack too heavily in one area only, leaving little or no room for other essentials. It would be foolhardy of me to leave on a desert journey with a pack full of winter clothing and no room left for the two-plus gallons of water I often need to carry. While warm clothing is an essential item for frequently frigid desert nights, too much of a good thing at the exclusion of other necessities can be a recipe for death. And something like death—at least an absence of real life—is often what many of us are left with because we don't have a good idea about what we should carry with us. My own life has often been marked by an overabundance of fear, leaving little room to feel grief or experience healthy and productive anger. We all likely know individuals dominated by their anger or immobilized by grief to the exclusion of anything else. As we conceive of life as a sojourn on this earth, it is vital that we learn to pack well as we move to our own House of Rain. We can now turn to these issues about what we might carry through the journey of life.

1

COMPLEXITY

I FOUND MYSELF ON a plane waiting to take off for a flight from Memphis to Cincinnati in May 2005 when I came across the following passage in Joe Simpson's book *This Game of Ghosts*.

> I hunched down immediately, facing into the slope and forcing all my weight on to my axe, trying to push it down, down into the very rock of the mountain ... The crescent-shaped wave of snow was almost upon me. I had thought maybe it was not so big; hoped it would brush over me. The wave punched me full in the chest, threw me over backwards, ripping the axe away effortlessly as I went down ... The snow, hundreds of tons of wet snow, swept to the left into a steep rocky-strewn ice gully. It curled and weaved its path from side to side, spewing snow up over boulders, rolling itself

over and over. I went with its fall, disoriented, lashing arms and legs, trying to control the force of it all. Smashing feet first into a large boulder in the gully bed, I was thrown up above the surging snow. I landed back in the gully, head down the slope, as the snow poured over the boulders, forcing me down against the ice. Wet snow jetted up my nostrils, packed my mouth, pushed me down harder. The rushing hiss of the avalanche faded, pressure pain built in my chest, sounds receded, a dull roaring in my head was like surf on a distant shingle beach, and all dimmed into grey shadows. (Simpson, 1994)

The fear these words produced was palpable; my heart raced as blood coursed through my body, tears welled up in my eyes, and adrenaline spiked in my system, seemingly getting stuck in my throat. It was as if I actually felt the words Simpson had written about an avalanche that had swept him twenty-five hundred feet off the Courtes in the Patagonian region of South America. I felt as if Simpson had actually been inside my head.

In March of 2005, just two months prior to this flight, I was climbing a fourteen-thousand-foot peak in the Tenmile Range of central Colorado with a man I worked with as a consultant. March 24 was a typical early spring day for the Rockies—cool temperatures punctuated by bursts of warm sunshine only to be obscured moments later by low clouds and blowing snow. I remember thinking that morning was the kind of weather that made a steep snow climb just as it should be.

I had met Jeff and his wife, Rene, in Denver for dinner the night before. We stayed up rather late that night, talking and getting better acquainted, which gave me little confidence that Jeff would make the trip to the mountain the next morning. Sometime around 11:00 p.m., I made my way to the hotel. Jeff and Rene traveled back to their home in Colorado Springs, where he would spend another hour or so gathering the necessary gear for the climb. We had arranged to meet at the Monte Christo Trailhead at 7:00 a.m., which meant a four-o'clock wake-up for both of us. Much to my surprise, Jeff was waiting for me at the trailhead that morning.

Rising only thirty to forty-five degrees in angle, the Cristo Couloir approach on the south side of Quandry Peak is not a particularly challenging climb even in winter. This makes the climb a good first outing and training climb for many. The approach follows a gently sloping road for nearly two miles leading to the shore of Blue Lake and the start of the climb proper. Jeff and I snowshoed up this first rise and then stowed them to don crampons. We started into the Cristo Couloir, a shallow, south-facing snow gully rising up the south face to within a few yards of the summit. Jeff was thoroughly enjoying the opportunity to be out on the mountain on a day like this, even if he was somewhat winded from the approach. As we strapped on our climbing gear and took ice ax in hand, Jeff expressed doubt as to his ability to summit that day. He encouraged me to climb at my own pace and meet him on the descent if necessary. I headed into the couloir at a smart pace. Jeff climbed behind, snapping photos and drinking in the high views of nearby ranges well above the tree line.

On a straightforward climb like this one, a climber quickly falls into a sort of rhythm, allowing one's mind to wander, especially when the person is climbing alone: step, step, plunge as you kick your crampons into the snow's crust for purchase and plunge your ice ax ahead of you as a sort of walking stick to lean on. I was soon in my pattern and free to consider my surroundings and appreciate the alternating periods of bright sun followed by an enveloping cloud of blinding snow only to clear out moments later. Near its midpoint, this couloir narrows, and I found the snow near the edges to be quite soft. It had started the melting process, drawing heat from the nearby rocks. I found myself continuously drawn to the middle of the gully, where the snow retained its solid crust, and it was much more comfortable for kicking steps with the crampons.

There is an interesting contour change near the route's midpoint as well. The slope below is somewhat steeper, and after one crosses onto higher elevations, it becomes somewhat obscured from view, like needing to walk to the very edge of a cliff in order to see what is directly below. After I crossed this change in angle, I soon lost sight of Jeff climbing below me. I turned my attention fully to the summit ridge in full view above. I remember reflecting on the ideal conditions of the day and the seemingly strange compulsion that had men like Jeff and me kicking steps up a mountain still bathed in winter and the compulsion to rise at 4:00 a.m. after a late night and walk into wind, sun, and snow, fighting fatigue in the legs and shortness of breath in the lungs.

Likely because of my thoughts on the ideal conditions of the day, it took me a moment to recognize the familiar "whump" that is the bane of every climber on high, snowy peaks. It is an unmistakable sound that registers directly in one's stomach and that marks the settling of one layer of snow on another. This sound generally indicates something very wrong is about to happen. At the time the sound came, I was at 13,700 feet—two thousand vertical feet above Blue Lake at a distance of about three fourths of a mile. When I heard it, I looked up to see an enormous fissure in the snow suddenly form, stretching from one side of the couloir to the other about thirty feet above me. It only took a fraction of a second for the layer of snow I had been climbing on with so much confidence moments before to begin its slide off the mountain. I was too close to the break, and the initial opening was too wide for me to avoid its path.

Many people involved in serious accidents attest to some sense of time stretching. Seconds can seem like minutes as all of one's senses are immediately employed in an effort to respond to the crisis. And although events may be unfolding very quickly, the moment can feel as if everything is moving in slow motion. When the snow began to succumb to the gravity pulling it downward to Blue Lake, I immediately turned my back to the slope, sat down, and prepared for a mountaineering self-arrest. This entails rolling over and letting one's body weight press down on an ice ax, burying the blade in the snow beneath you. I remember thinking there was no way this would turn into a full-scale avalanche. I fully expected the slide to stop at any moment. The slide didn't stop. In fact, more snow and increasing speed were being added to the melee every second. I soon realized I was indeed in an avalanche, one that was about to reach enormous proportions.

I was quickly drawn under the snow, and I lost all contact with light or any sense of up and down. Chaos was unleashed as the snow roared around me and did with me whatever it wanted. In his own avalanche account, Joe Simpson writes, "Swim. That's what everyone says. If you are caught in an avalanche, swim. No one told me that it would be like swimming through wet concrete, that surges of heavy wet snow would wrench and twist my body into agonizing contorted positions. *Swim*? The instruction manual writers must be bloody comedians" (Simpson, 1994).

There would be no swimming, no opening of a space for air, no clearing snow from my mouth, and no reaching toward the sky to try to give someone a clue as to my whereabouts. There was only mass confusion and a terrifying downhill ride I didn't want to be on. Items were swept from my hands and head, and I was tossed about like a slipper in a dog's mouth.

One of the more interesting things I realize in reflecting on the chaos of those moments was how clear my thinking seems to have been. It seemed as if I rather calmly processed my own demise numerous times. I have no idea how long it takes to ride sliding snow three quarters of a mile down a forty-degree slope, but it might as well have been a lifetime. As snow packed in my nostrils and mouth and breathing became impossible, I drew the conclusion—rather soberly, it seemed—that I would expire as many avalanche victims do, namely by asphyxiation, suffocating to death because air could not make its way to my lungs. I was soon aware of a squeezing sensation overtaking my body. Avalanches, despite occurring on snow and ice, can actually generate a great deal of heat, which often momentarily melts snow before it quickly consolidates into nearly impermeable blocks of ice. As the slide continued, the thought struck me that I might go as others had—crushed to death by the sheer weight of the snow and ice quickly entombing me.

Near the bottom of the Cristo Couloir and not far above Blue Lake, there is a cliff band that Jeff and I had skirted on the right in our ascent up Quandry Peak. To this day, I recall the completely lucid thought that as the slide continued, I was headed for this cliff band. My death seemed imminent at that point. I surmised that if I were tossed off this cliff band in the midst of this ever-increasing mass of snow and ice boulders, that I would surely be buried beneath many feet of impenetrable debris. My only hope was that the landing and burial would be quick and as painless as possible.

Ironically, it may have been this band of cliffs that ultimately saved my life. I was soon conscious of being airborne. I was no longer being drawn deeper under the snow toward the ground of the slope. Upon further reflection, it seems that when the avalanche blew me over this vertical rise, it gave the consolidating snow room to spread and actually lift the weight off of my body. It was at this point that the slow-motion highlight reel stopped and it seemed as if I were instantly in open air again, on my hands and knees, coughing and spitting snow from my lungs, gasping for air. I was on the frozen, flat surface of Blue Lake, two thousand vertical feet and three quarters of a mile below where the avalanche had broken. I had ridden this torrent down the entire course of the mountain, and it had spit me out at the very end as it lost its steam on the level surface of the lake.

When I regained my senses, my thoughts immediately turned to Jeff, whom I had not seen for nearly forty minutes before the slide had occurred. My hope was that he had perhaps started back to the vehicles or had climbed out of the couloir for the relative safety of the rocks lining the gully on both sides. I quickly scanned the slope above before I made my way to a small rise where I miraculously found a weak cell phone signal. It wasn't long before a helicopter dropped two search-and-rescue personnel with search dogs directly onto the mountain's slope. For the next two hours, I helped scour the mountainside among boulders of snow and ice as teams from three counties and at least four nearby ski areas were arriving to aid in the search. Jeff's body was found at the base of the couloir by a search dog. He had been buried under five feet of avalanche debris perhaps thirty yards from where I had emerged from the avalanche.

The autopsy report indicated that Jeff had likely died from a broken neck. It is admittedly small consolation, but my only comfort in this horrible tragedy is that Jeff's passing was quick and painless. At the time the avalanche occurred, Jeff was out of my sight, so he was likely at least a thousand feet below me and below the contour change I mentioned earlier. It appears that by the time the avalanche reached Jeff's position, it did so with such weight and force and so little notice that it likely struck him directly in front as it pushed off the higher slopes and broke Jeff's neck instantly as it bowled him over backward. The search-and-rescue team noted no indications of struggle where they had found Jeff's body. Jeff's funeral was held in Colorado Springs five days later, crowded with the people who had been deeply impacted by his short life.

The avalanche on Quandry Peak in March of 2005 was two thousand feet from top to bottom, four hundred feet wide and ten feet deep in some places combed by searchers. Researchers called this avalanche a "hard slab" avalanche, which was important for me to note. Avalanches frequently occur as "soft slab" slides immediately following a period of particularly heavy snow. Most typically, an avalanche occurs when a new snow load cannot adhere to a frozen and consolidated layer previously formed. Therefore, the load slides off, usually before the new layer has an opportunity to experience the cycles of thawing and freezing that tend to harden a layer. Hard slabs occur as a hardened, frozen, consolidated layer, one that may sit on a slope for an indefinite period of time, is broken from another layer underneath, a layer to which it hadn't actually adhered well. These kinds of avalanches are usually triggered by something on the slope, such as the weight of a climber. Hard slab slides clearly demonstrate a reality occurring on the surface which is not necessarily reflective of the conditions beneath. This is part of the reason the climbing conditions seemed so ideal that March day. The snow we were on was solid and provided good purchase, at least on the surface; however, the solid order on top was concealing an awaiting chaos below. I was clueless to this reality.

I certainly don't go into this account merely as another installment in the plethora of mountaineering incidents turned sour. There are too many records of epic climbs told much better than I could ever hope to. In the last decade in particular, the avalanche in 2005 that took Jeff's life and swept me off Quandry Peak has taken on enormous implications for me as a figure of life itself. In saying this, I intend no disrespect for Jeff's family as if the death of this superb young man is little more than my personal life lesson. I agree with Belden Lane when he says, "Only in devastating loss—beyond all security of language and identity, in despairing ever of obtaining the glory first sought—only then does a truth too wondrous to be grasped come rushing back out of the void" (Lane, 1998). The events of that spring day demonstrate the complexity that is life. What we may envision as solid order on the surface may actually be harboring a destructive chaos below. I have been caught in this "quandary," and I firmly believe that until life is understood and accepted as a continuous experience with complexity rather than as something strictly ordered or utterly chaotic, then we will struggle with who we are and how we can find our places in this epoch of history.

Over the past few decades, scientists working in the field of chaos theory have told us that the idea of complexity is woven into the very fabric of the universe. I am no scientist, but from what I understand of the theory, complexity continuously shows up not only in biological organisms but in social organizations as well. Consider the dynamics of a beehive. The queen bee, far from behaving as a ruling matriarch, does little other than give birth to sustain the hive. Bees apparently have no "central brain" that orchestrates the activities of the hive's members, and still, hives operate like well-oiled machines. Bees know their roles and communicate to other members of their community through complex dances to share work and keep the hive producing its nectar. Similarly, ant colonies, which communicate through pheromone trails, organize members through the collaborative efforts of the many individual ants. The point is that these systems are operating on a level of complexity. There is neither the order of some central mind directing all of the work nor the chaos of individual members running wild and doing their own thing without any direction.

The complexity of the human brain appears to operate on the same organic principles. Scientists have yet to find a single element of the brain that orders and controls all the operations of the various functions. No "central intelligence agency" dictates how the senses are to recognize and process inputs, how frequently the heart should beat, what to do in the case of a foreign invasion, or what memory looks like and how it affects us. Yet for all of the various activities occurring simultaneously in a healthy individual, these systems do not operate in a chaotic vacuum, causing the body or thoughts to fluctuate wildly as if they were fighting against one another or competing for necessary energy. Interestingly, the same dynamics of complexity show up in the social realities of an economy or a city. Economists have long been attempting to formulate a holistic theory for how our markets work, and many of the most brilliant minds in history often emerge with little more than frustration as anomalies continually surface. The economy appears to bow to no central ordering mind, and yet it has demonstrably throughout history been steered through cooperative efforts away from pure chaos. It is a system operating in the realm of complexity. Despite ongoing control-ordering attempts at designing and ruling cities, the same dynamics apply. Officials may attempt to lay out cities according to a master plan, but throughout history, enclaves of citizens and immigrants shape urban life in ways never anticipated but still work for those on the ground. Although pockets of city life appear completely ordered or utterly chaotic, overall urban life has worked itself out in a layer of complexity—that fine line between order and chaos.

Complexity is important to understand partially because of the embedded idea of "fitness landscapes." Not only is this a picturesque means of extending our metaphor for how wild places lay over healthy lives, but it also expounds what the theory tells us about how healthy organisms and organizations are formed. A fitness landscape can be pictured as a vast mountain range consisting of peaks and valleys, some visible, others still out of one's vantage point. Biological and social systems tend to order themselves so as to climb to sustainable levels of what they see as thriving health, pictured as an ascent of a nearby peak. Reaching a particular peak, however—as any climber well knows—often opens a greater view of other distant and higher peaks. For such organisms, the "order" used to reach the first peak is likely not sufficient for an ascent of another higher peak of fitness. The resulting action then is usually some form of chaos appearing as a descent into a valley before they gather strength for another summit bid. This becomes a sort of dance then—alternating epochs of order and chaos as organisms and organizations move to greater fitness peaks. Too much of either movement stilts healthy advance. Too much order may freeze one on a fitness peak much lower than one could have attained otherwise while the presence of unmitigated chaos will never allow one to progress out of the valley. The point at which the greatest fitness peak is reached, therefore, is the knife's edge between order and chaos—what scientists call complexity. This is the sweet spot between overly stultifying order and utterly destructive chaos.

One beautiful summer outing for me and a couple of friends entailed a climb up Colorado's Huron Peak followed the next day by planned ascents of Belford, Missouri, and Oxford—three fourteen-thousand-foot peaks in Colorado's Sawatch Range. We began the second day with a straightforward ascent up 14,067-foot Missouri Mountain from our camp on the Lake Fork at around 10,800 feet. The climb up the West Ridge is fairly straightforward and entails little more than a long walk from timberline through grassy slopes and occasional scree fields before one snakes around rock towers near the summit. When a person reaches the summit of Missouri Mountain, he or she is treated to a real-life lesson in fitness landscapes as numerous other thirteen- and fourteen-thousand-foot peaks rise into sight, towering over Missouri and Belford gulches and numerous high basins. The rock-covered escarpments of Iowa Peak, Emerald Peak, Mount Belford, Pecks Peak, and Mount Oxford dominate the horizon, and all require descents onto high passes or into falling basins in order to move between.

Our agenda for the day called for a descent of Missouri's East Ridge to Elkhead Pass at 13,220 feet before we moved up the gentle slopes of Belford's south side. A prominent guidebook on Colorado's Fourteeners describes the route this way: "This route's Class 4 rating disguises a serious and dangerous climb. What should be Missouri's premier mountaineering route is so rotten that it is relegated to this author's nightmares" (Roach, 1999). My partners and I spent hours attempting to negotiate ledges, steep buttresses, and rubble-filled gullies in an attempt to keep the climbing to the nontechnical class-four rating, which we seemed to rarely accomplish that afternoon. After what seemed like an eternity poised on the edge of utter chaotic climbing, we found ourselves standing on Elkhead Pass, looking up at the high slopes of Mount Belford. It was certainly a lesson in complexity as a fitness landscape was opened before us, one that required a complex balance between the order of established trails and the chaos of rotten, technical rock in order to move among the existing landscape. Moving to a higher peak required a careful descent that would only allow our movement to a higher vantage point when we successfully accomplished the task at hand.

I find in this science such an important and compelling theory because it reflects so much of life so well for so many of us: emotionally, spiritually, intellectually, and primarily physically. We all tend to move through periods of life we can easily identify as periods of order or times of chaos. I know my own life has fluctuated between those poles as I have searched for that balance of living in the complexity of existence.

Like many of my contemporaries, I left home at eighteen to begin college—away from what I convinced myself was an oppressive order on my development. I began my freshman year of college at a small private school in eastern Nebraska, far enough from southwest Wyoming, to begin to do what I wanted with life. School was paid for that first year through a large scholarship, so the student loan I applied for was simply money for me to spend as I saw fit in shaping my own kind of life. Sparing the details, the chaos of that first year culminated in a hitchhiking trip to Reno, Nevada, for spring break. Despite my state of mind at the time, I was lucid enough to recognize the chaos my life was quickly becoming. In hitchhiking across the Nevada desert, Jason and I were treated to an entire lifetime's worth of education as we were offered rides from individuals who had spent decades of their own lives spinning off into perpetual chaos. I felt at the time as if I were being treated to a vision of my own future, were I to continue traveling this road. There was nothing healthy about my landscape—only a desert valley as far as I could see. I needed to restore some sense of order.

I made a change of venue to begin my sophomore year, and this served as a necessary corrective for me at that time. This relocation seemed to serve me well for the next decade and a half. For the next three years of college and three years of graduate school following, I poured myself into the doctrines and lifestyles of conservative Evangelical Christianity. It was a system of intense order. For six years, I was engaged in ancient language studies so that I could translate and accurately understand biblical text in order to extract answers to life's questions and pass those answers on to others. I took numerous courses in systematic theology. I was taught that God and his doctrines and expectations could be fully systematized in order for us to fully understand our place and purpose in his world. Through studying apologetics, I was supposed learn the knowledge to answer every critic and the tools to stave off every confusion about doctrine. Issues were black-and-white, and answers were clear for those smart enough—or learned enough—to figure everything out. Life was a grand system of order with everything in its place.

During this period, I was also immersed in a culture that ordered the life of the mind by lifestyle choices with the following statements: "These things are always good." "These things are always bad." "One should always do this, and one should never do that." "Drink this, but don't drink that." It all seemed so straightforward. For my own stage of life and other twentysomethings around me, this was all intended to direct us to some kind of perfect plan, specifically God's will for life. If we knew enough and towed the line well enough in our personal conduct, then we were sure to find our ways into some kind of grand scheme where we would know our places and find the perfect ordered context for us to thrive in. I spent nearly a decade convincing others of this perspective as I planted new churches in rural communities and then helped others do the same as a sort of "church-planting consultant."

I don't desire to be misunderstood as being overly critical of the entirety of conservative evangelicalism. There is much in this approach to be commended, and its order allowed me to climb out of the valley of my own chaos to a sort of fitness peak. At the same time, I have become convinced that this is not the whole story and likely not a completely accurate picture of how life has been designed. I began to harbor some serious questions about the inherent order in the system I was perpetuating. Religion and spirituality, perhaps especially the kind drawn from the pages of the Bible and the life of Jesus, seems far more complex than this ordered system I had inherited. Throughout the accounts of not only biblical figures but men and women throughout history, there is a great deal of variety in how God deals with people. Job's story comes to mind as does the death of Jesus and the subsequent martyrdom or most of his closest followers. To simply assume life will be grand and perfect happiness found in adhering to certain doctrines seems disingenuous. Jesus himself said that God causes the rain to fall on the just and unjust alike. Pre-Jesus prophets must have seemed scandalous at times as they spoke of how God intervened in the lives of outsiders and "Gentiles" and even at times used them in decisively instrumental ways to accomplish some purpose.

In drafting his own apologetics for the existence and grandeur of the Hebrew/Christian concept of God, Anselm is credited with positing the idea of God as "that than which nothing greater can be conceived." The idea immediately places the reality of God in the realm of the complex. Our words and ideas of the absolute must always come up short and be humbled at the doorstep of mystery, which even the great doctrine-former apostle Paul attested to. The Bible was written by a

SOJOURN

prescientific people whose intent was not to answer all of our questions of strict order. A collection of stories, poetry, and letters to individual people in specific locales does not constitute a road map or scientific and systematic treatise. This is not meant to devalue these writings, only to demonstrate the level of complexity on which this spirituality is formed and should be practiced.

Being involved on the forefront of forming new church communities, the order I was striving for as an organization simply did not seem to mesh with reality. The programs and practices my context sought to perpetuate seemed to create a club environment we could be comfortable in with people who looked like us, smelled like us, and used the same language we used. Spiritual contexts shared as a community—a church— should serve to make us better neighbors in a messy and complex world, not simply perpetuate our own exclusivity. There were also inevitably many conservative requirements on lifestyle issues. Some of these lifestyle expectations such as what to listen to, what one could eat and drink, what language was appropriate were not tenable from a biblical perspective. They simply served to create order for our own context where those in our club could be kept in check based on the list of do's and don'ts. Many of Jesus' own words are invariably complex, and we do the founder a disservice to bring our own twenty-first-century requirement for order to bear on his words instead of allowing them to disturb us in their complexity.

The science of chaos tells us that order may lead an organization or organism to a fitness peak, but that peak may not be the optimum height in any given landscape. At times order may actually keep one from moving to a greater peak. Without a grasp of the relationship between chaos, order and complexity, my own sense of order—not being a sufficient fitness peak to sustain life—began to degenerate again toward chaos. I left the professional ministry and took a job as a roughneck in western Colorado. The order I had built my life around for the previous seventeen years was unraveling, and my identity was coming apart with it. I found myself again in the throes of chaos. I nearly lost all of the most important things in my life during a particularly dark and aimless year which followed soon after. I hope to be emerging now toward a higher peak with a new appreciation for the health of the complex.

This is why the avalanche on Quandry Peak in 2005 holds such a prominent place in my thinking about life. On the slope that day, there appeared to be sufficient order on the surface. That order soon broke into a cascade of chaos that usually took other lives with it. For me, life wasn't as straightforward and the future wasn't as laid out as I had imagined. The point is that each of us needs to recognize the movement toward a high peak on our own fitness landscapes. In order to move to optimum health, we need to embrace the complexity of life and avoid the dangerous poles of trying to order or control all of life on the one hand or allowing it to degenerate into the chaos of wanton pleasure on the other.

It is part of the human condition (as with any organism or organization) to want to discover the highest peak on our own fitness landscape. Many of us, however, harbor a great deal of confusion about the means of discovering where such a high peak might really be found. Zac has been my climbing partner for over ten years. Early on in our climbing efforts, we seemed to have particular issues with the peaks in the Crestones in the

Sangre de Christo Range of southern Colorado. One Fourth of July, we headed up the east side of the range to climb Crestone Needle. Before we left the vehicle at around 11,500 feet, we briefly looked at the route in a guidebook and headed for the mountain. When we reached a high basin, everything seemed totally unfamiliar, and we soon found ourselves off route and on top of Broken Hand Peak instead. Fortunately, the day was not totally lost as we simply followed a high ridgeline to a point from which we could summit the Needle. Later that same year in October, we started out for Crestone Peak from the west side of the range. The summit of these peaks is often not visible from below, and we overshot our goal and found ourselves on the high ridge that stretched from Crestone Needle to Crestone Peak—a ridge I vowed I would never do when I had viewed it from the Needle in July. The ridge is one of Colorado's four great fourteener traverses and consists of class-four broken climbing up and down a half-mile ridge of steep exposure. Fortunately, we made the summit and survived to tell the story.

Life too often feels like you are wandering long, broken, exposed ridges, not always able to discern the point at which you hope to arrive. Many of us then alternate between our own order or control and the chaos of a life virtually out of control. We must make space to embrace the complex nature of our existence. Failing to secure such space, many of us spend a great deal of time and energy attempting to order and program confusion, weight, fear, and suffering out of our lives. It is not unusual for people to believe that they can have their personal space, career, conduct, and feelings in order and that as a result, tragedy cannot really affect them. The right income to provide the right vehicle and the right house in the right neighborhood will insulate me from any confusion or chaos. The right belief system, fitness program, and lawn fertilizer will provide the necessary order for my peak fitness. Chaos can be gated out or sent to a home far away.

Still, others may actually use chaos itself to cover up the naturalness of the complex nature of existence beneath a plethora of material goods or artificial sensations brought about through various drugs—legal or otherwise. It is possible to even use other lives to distract us from the frustration of our own. H. G. Wells is reported to have said, "When you can go through contemporary life fudging and evading, indulging and slacking, never really hungry nor frightened nor passionately stirred—your first real contact with primary and elemental necessities will be the sweat of your deathbed." We begin with the concept of complexity because this serves as the organizing principle behind our ability to grasp the meaning of weight and fear in life on our way to integration.

What would it mean at this stage of life to embrace and swim in complexity? I believe it would at least partially mean that we stop trying to explain everything, to answer everything, to micromanage all the various aspects of life—our own or those around us. This seems to be an issue, especially with men. Often my wife will approach me with some kind of struggle, and as my immediate response, I want to fix whatever is wrong with whatever kind of solution I can come up with. Colleen may not even need something "fixed" but may simply need to air an issue. I know that I often lack answers or solutions and my first response is to get defensive in order to attempt to provide some cover for not knowing. Not everything can be immediately explained or answered from our limited perspective and finite understanding. This is part of what makes life the mess it often is. Our control issues are not limited to our own lives, either. For too many approaching life's middle years, life seems out of control and confusing; dreams go unfulfilled, and expectations stubbornly refuse to be met. In an attempt to maintain the appearance of order, some may try to maintain undue control over their children's lives. This is a way to convince ourselves that we can still salvage this chaos, but it is also terribly unfair to our children who simply become our personal conduits for a second run at life.

Sometimes we simply need to learn to be okay with the mystery. If the very Creator of life has determined to somehow maintain at least portions of his being as mysteries, then it is unlikely that we will ever fully understand everything about existence. The sooner we grasp this perspective, the sooner we can move to balance our own constricting order and uncontrollable chaos. There is not likely to be an answer for everything we encounter in life. After the avalanche, I found it difficult to understand why the promising life of a young man would be taken and mine would be spared. How could I have survived two thousand feet of slide while Jeff was killed in barely half that distance? Many people had nice things to say to me and attempted to provide some answers, but most of this remains a mystery today. I understand that people mean well, but when we learn to live in the complexity of life, then *that* is something significant to share with one another rather than simply nice words. We seem to have this uncontrollable urge to say things that can answer everything and to figure everything out. I do not believe we should give up trying to live and make sense of life, but why don't we cease to refuse to move forward until all of our accounts are in order and the future is secure for us?

Moving into the moment of complexity is actually like applying brakes to life—it's like a movement by way of anti-movement. This is a pause in our flight from the confusion of life. Typically we have learned to combat such confusion by either building a strict set of structures to govern all of life (order) or by throwing off all structure which might hinder us (chaos). Becoming comfortable with the ideas of complexity allows us to cultivate a sane moment when we might consider how hardship, suffering, privation, and liminality could have value when it comes to learning to thrive in our existence rather than always evading these things or attempting to engineer them out of our context. I do not intend to sound like I have this dialed in already, but what I do have is a great teacher, particularly the outdoor life.

A few years ago, two climbers set out into the Wind River Mountains of Wyoming to attempt an "enchainment," a long climbing effort that links multiple peaks together in a single push, often running into dozens of miles, thousands of feet of elevation gained and lost, and even days without sleep. One of these climbers found himself deep in the wilderness, too sick and too exhausted to continue climbing. His climbing partner received a letter a few weeks following the expedition and submitted this portion to *Outside Magazine*:

> It may have been piling on too many straws, or it may have merely been a weakened emotional state. I may never know. But it doesn't matter. Everyone has such moments. Life suddenly robs you of your focus right when the task before you demands everything you have to give. The pressure mounts and you crack, not

from pegging the meter, but from operating too near the red line. These are the trips that shape individuals and partnerships, the fire that refines our metal and reveals our weaknesses and impurities within. Mark, we must not delude ourselves by thinking we do not possess such weaknesses. On the contrary, I pray we always encourage each other to live in a manner that exposes them. (Jensen, 2002)

Wild places and the purposeful "pilgrimages" to wilderness can serve as schools for learning to live in the complexity of life away from such experiences. An Inuit shaman was quoted in *Across Arctic America* as saying, "All wisdom is only to be learned far from the dwellings of men, out in the great solitude, and is only to be attained through suffering. Privation and suffering are the only things that can open the mind of man to those things which are hidden from others" (Rasmussen, 1999). This is the point of Joseph Conrad's vision. The wilderness opens us to ourselves and to what is often hidden deep within. We run a great risk by trying to fudge our way through life without gaining some self-knowledge. Far too many lives attest to this. Countless individuals, perhaps most often men, enter the middle years of life and experience a sort of implosion or dissolution as the buried elements of the self begin to spill out of cracks in destructive ways. Wilderness pilgrimages can help us continuously live in ways that expose us to ourselves and surface the complexity of life.

Our various responses to hardship and suffering reveal areas of particular importance. Despite the best efforts of any of us to program and order insulated lives, we are never able to completely exempt ourselves from the realities of suffering in life. Because the knife-edge of complexity is our best place for growth between the order and the chaos, we learn to do something with our hardship rather than ignore it or allow it to destroy us. There is actually great value in learning to walk into these complex life situations. Malcolm Muggeridge once said,

> Contrary to what might be expected, I look back on experiences which at the time seemed especially desolating and painful with particular satisfaction. Indeed, I can say with complete truthfulness that everything I have learned in my seventy-five years in this world, everything that has truly enhanced and enlightened my existence, has been through affliction and not through happiness, whether pursued or attained.

My first exposure to winter climbing occurred many years ago on a fourteen-thousand-foot peak in the Sangre de Christo Mountains in southern Colorado. A large group of us headed out for Willow Lake at the base of Challenger Point two days before Christmas. I had little idea what was in store for me. Up to this point, I had only been climbing these peaks for about six months and only in warmer summer weather. The intense cold and shortened days of winter seemed to conspire against us. We had packed Cornish game hens for dinner our night out, and they were still frozen solid when we reached Willow Lake. Our gas stoves had a difficult time priming in the intense cold, and they often erupted into a ball of flame as gas instead of vapor poured out. We decided to sleep on the frozen top of the lake because of its level surface, and we spent a long, unsettled night listening to the ice heave and crack. Our malfunctioning stoves kept us from melting snow for water, so Zac and I climbed with a small half liter of water between the two of us. We chose a snow- and rock-covered ridgeline to ascend, and we were met by a cornice-covered knife-edge summit ridge. Nothing seemed to work out as we had planned, and the wind was intense during the climb as it battered against our bid for the summit. For whatever reason, I thoroughly enjoyed the exposure to the elements, and we began to repeat our annual "Christmas trip" to other peaks for many years. Despite the discomfort, the effort was somehow worth each minute, and I found myself hooked.

I mentioned before that Zac and I have at times had issues with finding the "standard" route up a peak or an entrance to or exit from a Utah slot canyon, never entirely convinced we are where the guidebooks say we should be. I believe I shoulder the bulk of responsibility in this case. I have stubbornly refused to utilize a GPS device because I am still not convinced that I should always know exactly where I am. I realize many would cringe at this admission, but I refuse to believe this is really such a bad thing. Getting sidetracked from a standard route has never been an issue with me because I have been able to see a lot of country and a great deal more places than a more "standard" and orderly approach would allow. If one has some competence in travel and survival, then getting off trail (and I have always avoided the word and idea of being "lost") is not really an issue.

This is precisely how wilderness layers over life as a learning metaphor. Can we find the beauty in a complex world when we find ourselves off the ordered path we had established and planned on walking through in our old age? How do we understand our place in the world when life throws us a

57

curveball? When that canyon or that mesa isn't where the map or guidebook says it should be, what should we do? If we can understand complexity, we might be able to continue to revel in life and believe we are actually making progress toward a better fitness landscape precisely because of some confusion or hardship. One would think I could have learned this before my own order gave way to utter chaos in 2009. However, it's the very complexity of life that makes it so beautiful and worthwhile. This is precisely where too many people get stuck in life. They have no idea what to do with their own existences when at fortysomething, they find their lives have stubbornly refused to bow to a preconceived order.

Zac and I accidently bypassed an exit out of the North Middle Fork of Robber's Roost Canyon after we descended the Not MindBender Slot in Utah one gorgeous afternoon. What turned out to be our exit seemed so unlikely at the time that we ended up hiking for hours up the Middle Fork of Robber's Roost only to have to turn back and recover miles of canyon. This scenario has happened more than once. I still refuse to get frustrated by these lapses in navigational judgment because without such "mistakes," I would have missed miles of beautiful canyon scenery that I might not otherwise have seen in my lifetime. I believe that at some point, most of us find that life is not as straightforward as we thought it would be and the "guidebooks" are not always easy to follow. They don't always line up to the path we find ourselves on. I am finding that to be okay, though, because healthy life really is found on that small edge called complexity which is where we strike the balance between order and chaos.

In her book *Red: Passion and Patience in the Desert*, Terry Tempest-Williams does a beautiful job of presenting the idea of how landscape and wild places lay over life as metaphors full of lessons in seeking to make the best of life in this world. At one point, she writes,

> Just when you believe in your own sense of place, plan on getting lost. It's not your fault—blame it on Coyote [Navajo: Ma'ii, the one never to be taken for granted]. The terror of the country you thought you knew bears gifts of humility. The landscape that makes you vulnerable also makes you strong. This is the bedrock of Southern Utah's beauty: Its chameleon nature according to light and weather and season encourages us to make peace with our own contradictory nature. The trickster quality of the canyons is coyote's cachet. (Tempest-Williams, 2001)

Grasping and determining to live on the edge of complexity is a setup for the other important elements of life that follow. Knowing that hardship, suffering, and privation add something integral to a thorough existence and help us add weight to life, walk in an ever-present fear, and emerge as fully integrated and present human beings. If we can learn to walk this fine line between stultifying order and destructive chaos, we will find ourselves on a climb to a higher fitness peak. In order to get there, however, we'll have to add more weight.

2

WEIGHT

STANDING AT 13,804 feet, Gannett Peak marks the high point in the state of Wyoming, surpassing the far more popular Grand Teton by thirty-four feet. Named for Henry Gannett, the chief topographer of the Hayden Survey and later in charge of topographic surveying for the United Stated Geologic Survey, Gannett was first climbed in 1922 by Arthur Tate and Floyd Stahlnaker. Ironically, Henry Gannett likely never actually set eyes upon his namesake mountain, which may be a testament to the peak's shy and secluded nature. Not visible from any road, Gannett entails the longest approach of any high peak in the lower forty-eight. This, the presence of continuous snow cover, and five flanking glaciers have earned Gannett the reputation as the most alpine peak in the American Rockies.

One typical approach to Gannett Peak entails over twenty miles from Elkhart Park above Pinedale to the Titcomb Basin south of the peak. The approach is a series of trails linked together and is a continuous struggle over ascents to passes followed by descents to high lake basins. After climbers reach the remote Titcomb Basin, they must ascend Bonney Pass at 12,800 feet only to subsequently lose most of their elevation gain in descending onto the Dinwoody Glacier before they make their way over to the final approach up the Gooseneck Glacier on Gannett's northeast aspect. Climbers approaching from this southern route typically give themselves five days to summit the peak: two days to pack into Titcomb Basin, one day to summit, and two days for the return to Elkhart Park. Likely because of youthful ambition, Zac and I planned three days for one summit bid in August of 2003. This really wasn't considered a superhuman feat however, as the peak has been climbed via a continuous twenty-six-hour push from trailhead to trailhead.

For years, my approach to a trip such as this was fairly easy to predict. I would push too hard for too long and wind up paying a heavy price. Zac and I fairly raced through the trails to the Titcomb Basin, rarely even pausing to either eat or drink. By the time we reached our high camp at the base of Bonney Pass late on the first day, I was severely dehydrated and utterly spent. Zac cooked us a meal of some kind of pasta and sauce, which I attempted to eat, knowing I needed some nourishment. About halfway through the meal, my body rejected it, and everything came back out. Despite desperately needing food and water, my body couldn't deal with the digestion on top of attempting to care for the effects of my dehydration. With much cajoling, Zac convinced me to finish the second half of my meal and finally keep some liquid down. One of my favorite pictures to this day is a photo Zac snapped of me staring off into nowhere, looking pale and miserable as I sat with a pot of tomato-covered pasta in one hand.

If the hard push of the first day and the personal wall I had hit late in the day weren't bad enough, we had to rise early the next morning and begin the arduous ascent to the top of Bonney Pass. Then we discovered how far the drop was onto the Dinwoody Glacier. We had to finish all of this before we could even begin to make our way around a rock escarpment just to get on the Gooseneck Glacier, where the actual climb of Gannett Peak would begin. I was already shot, and the thought that we would have to again make this climb back up the pass on our return already weighed on my mind in the early morning hours. Before long, Zac and I found ourselves on the glaciers on Gannett's north side, negotiating small crevasses and searching for a likely route up the Gooseneck. Finally, with the summit ridge in view, we had only one final steep couloir to ascend before we could stand on the highest point in Wyoming. At the base of this final gain, however, we found ourselves stopped by an enormous bergschrund, a gaping hole stretching from cliff wall to cliff wall this late in the season. A bergschrund consists of a large crevasse that is created when a glacier pulls away from the vertical rock sections of a peak. Because we wanted to travel fast and light on this attempt, Zac and I had left ropes and anchors behind, and we were now stopped cold within sight of the summit. Somewhat dejectedly, we began our long slog back over Bonney Pass to retrieve our gear and begin the long trek back to the vehicle.

All of those miles, the self-imposed suffering, the ascending and descending and negotiating—all that finished only to return home without having reached the summit. As we have talked about that trip through the years, however, there is never a hint of regret from either Zac or me. Zac found those areas of the Wind Rivers reminiscent of his time in Nepal. I continue to count the Titcomb Basin as one of the top two places I have had the privilege to visit. As with many hard trips we've taken, Zac and I emerged believing every step was worth the experience, not because of a summit we could mark off and probably even in spite of an arbitrary foot of land we might call a summit. Those trips, we realize, are worthwhile precisely because of their difficulty. They tend to add substance to life through the suffering. The hard things tend to grant a substantial weight to our existence, a weight necessary to be able to experience and enjoy a full life.

Whether we spend any time in the backcountry or not, our tendency is to approach life like a seasoned backpacker or accomplished alpine climber, continuously seeking to lighten our loads, to travel with as few encumbrances as possible, and to live light, fast, and free. While this certainly doesn't apply to our consumptive lifestyle and thinking about possessions in America, it does apply to what we allow to weigh on our hearts, minds, and souls. We want to be carefree and stress-free, and therefore, we find ourselves not all that attached to the issues and lives of other people or important events or crises in our world. We often lack empathy for our neighbors and probably even the pain in our own extended family. In seeking to lighten our loads through life, which has taken on a form of virtue in our culture, we are required to detach from our world and retreat behind closed doors and gated communities.

When I was leading backpacking camps for high school and college students in the 1990s, I would typically carry an ancient and oversized, external-frame Jansport pack that I had purchased for one dollar at a garage sale. Apparently, its previous owner had tired of carrying this behemoth into the backcountry. As is often the case, I tended to fill every nook and cranny in the enormous pack simply because I had the space. I felt largely responsible for the groups of thirty or more who would show up, often with little or no backcountry experience, so I would load up this mammoth pack with everything I thought might be missed or left behind. I spent weeks and countless miles bent under the enormous weight. Things are much different now that I have availed myself of ultralight gear and solo travel into the wilderness. I still find myself learning about weight all the time, though. For years, the only rope I carried to descend Utah's slot canyons was a sixty-meter dynamic dry rope of eleven-millimeter gauge—it was the only rope I owned. When I met four guys from Wyoming headed into a slot I was planning to travel by myself and joined their descent, I experienced the joy of carrying and rappelling off an eight-millimeter static rope. Those kinds of trips to wild places make considerations of "weight" vital.

Unlike a backpacking trip or an alpine climb, when we seek to "lighten up" in life, it's likely we're missing something crucial. To move through life as light and unencumbered as possible is not the same virtue that it is for a climber. We require a certain weightiness because with weight comes significance. In the Hebrew Scriptures, the word for one of the most fundamental characteristics of Yahweh is *cabod*, which literally means "weight." The word is most frequently translated as "glory" and points to the fact that God has substance and therefore must be acknowledged and responded to.

The best way I know to illustrate this difficult concept is to refer the reader to the picturesque discussion in C. S. Lewis's *The Great Divorce*. Lewis presents a vision of a busload of people being transported from hell to heaven. When they arrive, the passengers find that they are mere ghosts in the midst of utter reality. "Walking proved difficult. The grass hard as diamonds to my unsubstantial feet, made me feel as if I were walking on wrinkled rock." The inhabitants of this strange and surreal land were absolutely solid by contrast. "The earth shook under their tread as their strong feet sank into the turf" (Lewis, 1946). The story consists of a series of interactions between the ghosts and the solid people who continuously endeavor to convince their guests of the good reality of being in a solid and substantial place. "Will you come with me to the mountains?" one of the inhabitants asks a ghost. "It will hurt at first, until your feet are hardened. Reality is harsh to the feet of shadows."

Near the midpoint of the story, the narrator is met by a teacher who deigns to explain to the confused guest some of the realities of the strange country. Their conversation is punctuated by scenes involving conversations between other ghosts and the solid inhabitants of what is presented as heaven. It soon becomes apparent that the ghostlike people lack substance because of their attachment to experiences on earth, experiences that keep them locked in unreality. There are figures that have defined life by their careers, their pride, their grief, their wounds and shame—all elements that keep individuals appearing as one-dimensional and therefore lacking substance. The primary issue for all the light and unsubstantial beings is soon revealed to be a tenacious attachment to a particular expression of life. Pleasure, education, reputation, caregiving—they are among the expressions of life which at first seem legitimate pursuits, but which eventually degenerate into poor substitutes for a life of actual substance. The passion of a painter or explorer, the love of a mother, the pursuit of a scholar—these are all elements that come to consume life, and people pursue them not for their own end but merely because the pursuit or expression is all an individual can define life by. Lewis's teacher explains this idea through the example of what he calls "the sensualist." "The sensualist, I'll allow ye, begins by pursuing a real pleasure, though a small one … But the time comes on when, though the pleasure becomes less and less and the craving fiercer and fiercer, and though he knows that joy can never come that way, yet he prefers to joy the mere fondling of unappeasable lust and would not have it taken from him" (Lewis, 1946).

The point is that there are many legitimate pursuits in life and emotional responses to our circumstances. At times, however, these can become all-encompassing for us and leave us missing too many other aspects of the self which would round out existence. We then potentially become one-dimensional beings and lose out on what might build in us a substance or weight. We all run the risk in our contemporary situation of becoming only one-dimensional through our possessions, our overrun sensuality, our overactive intellect, or even our overbearing grief. Working in the oil field for a number of years, where wages are unusually high for blue-collar labor, I have met many people who do little other than work. In the midst of making a great deal of money, however, there seems to be little or no time left to enjoy the fruits of one's labors or to pause and appreciate the beauty and variety of the world we inhabit. Others bent only on the sensual in life through sexual encounters, gluttony, or artificial highs typically miss the balancing lessons to be found only through the pain and suffering in the reality of our world. My grandmother appeared to harbor and cultivate a grief throughout her life because of the early and tragic death of a daughter. It was rare for me to witness her finding joy in life or people around her. A life of substance and weight is able to see beyond the immediate and experience the solidity of a full spectrum of emotions, endeavors, attentions, and activities.

There is an obvious point of connection in the concept of weight with what has already been said about complexity and the layering metaphor of wild places. In stark contrast to the life mired in chaos, which feels little or at least makes everything a cover and distraction from feeling, and the life of extreme and compulsive order, which would engineer existence so that one could insulate or isolate him or herself from unpleasant experiences, to add weight to our lives would be to embrace the complexity which endues our world. Joseph Conrad had just this vision of wilderness in mind because in a modern and industrial world, the wild parts of our world can lead us to primal expressions and emotions that we typically fear. In important ways, we have lost the ability to deal with ourselves. This is the picture of many of the ghosts in *The Great Divorce* and too many of us who get stuck in what is only lightness.

In *All the Live Little Things*, a novel by Wallace Stegner, one finds the narrator, a retired literary agent, in the midst of a process of appreciating complexity and thereby adding layers of weight to his life. Joe Allston has retired to a quiet rural neighborhood in the hills of California in an attempt to relax and enjoy his last years on earth. Joe is pictured early as a man who likes his order: meticulously landscaping his piece of land, rooting out moles and gophers that would inevitably mar his property, and often raging at the scars of roads on a hillside across from his property that wreck his otherwise pristine view. Allston soon finds his quiet world turned upside down as he acquires two new neighbors: a young housewife and mother who is bent on appreciating the wild and natural beauty of the native species of the California hills and a beatnik squatter who takes up residence on Allston's property and surfaces memories of his own troubled son, who has been dead for many years.

The novel is more than worth its weight because of the movement it pictures Joe Allston making from a person who is insulated and emotionally unattached to one who appreciates and embraces the weight and complexity of his world. The change occurs as he interacts with his new neighbors. The squatter, Jim Peck, reminds Allston far too much of his own son, whom he never knew how to deal with because of the disorder and complexity the young man would bring into Allston's otherwise pristine world. His interactions with the young housewife next door, however, make the greatest impact on Joe Allston, and these scenes illustrate very clearly a life learning to acquire weight. When Marian, her husband, and her daughter move to a nearby cottage, the Allstons are immediately drawn to the feisty, full-of-life personality of the Catlains and take Marian in like a daughter. It is when Marian is diagnosed with an incurable form of cancer and begins to prepare herself for death that the real lessons for Joe Allston begin. Through her dying and her ongoing appreciation for the small things in life, Allston begins to acquire an appreciation for the weight and complexity of life. At one point, Marian says to Joe, "Don't you get pleasure—satisfaction—no, pleasure it really is—out of all the rough, hot, cold, scratchy, uncomfortable things" (Stegner, 1967)? It is significant that this statement comes from a woman in the painful throes of dying, and it begins to break down Joe's one-dimensional, orderly, and light existence, which he had spent his entire life trying to control and cultivate like a perfect garden, one free from the confusion of the weeds and moles in the rest of the world.

Marian then quotes part of the poem "To Earthward" by Robert Frost, which she had memorized.

> When stiff and sore and scarred
>
> I take away my hand
>
> From leaning on it hard
>
> In grass and sand,
>
> The hurt is not enough:
>
> I long for weight and strength
>
> To feel the earth as rough
>
> To all my length

To actually long for a weight and a substance of life that would allow us to actually feel the important elements of our existence is a rare thing. Most of us only know how to live in the lightness of our context—doing what we can through work or pleasure to keep from feeling the rough reality of our world. Our lightness will eventually lead to our undoing as we butt up against reality, which requires a sort of substance to endure.

The idea that it is a rare thing to long for a weighty life that has developed through an actual engagement with trying circumstances needs some qualification. I believe that many people naturally intuit the value of what is required of us to move into lives of substance, even if they are often more inclined to avoid the situations that would grant this much-needed substance to life. As Zac and I planned more difficult outings like our trip to Gannett Peak, we found ourselves at times overwhelmed by people in our circle wanting to travel with us. Neither of us was inclined to sugarcoat the nature of these trips as we would be brutally honest in our portrayal of how cold, hard, long, and difficult these outings were, particularly on our annual Christmas climbs. Apart from any advertising or promotion of our plans, Zac and I would inevitably be sought out by groups wanting to add something of substance to their otherwise comfortable lives by joining us in the backcountry. Even if we often fail to engage with the weight of daily life, many people somehow know that whatever adds substance through some kind of enforced, controlled suffering is actually a good thing.

Zac has not only served as my personal climbing partner for many years but also played a vital role as a partner in the backpacking endeavors I led for high school and college-aged students for many years from the San Luis Valley of Colorado. One July, we had an unusually high number of participants, which required us to split the students into two traveling groups. We all began at the Cottonwood Trailhead on the west side of the Sangre de Christo wilderness and traveled to a camp in Horsethief Basin. I took one group farther onto Cotton Lake and across a high pass to finish our week in the Rito Alto Basin. The plan was for Zac to take his group north to South Branch Lake and then cross the spine of the range to descend Major Creek. This second group had the misfortune of facing a three-thousand-foot ascent out of Horsethief Basin with a week's worth of gear loaded on their backs. High above the timberline, Banjo Lake was supposed to lead them to the Crossover Trail and then South Branch Lake. Because of the arduous nature of the climb out of Cottonwood Creek, the group decided to forgo the food drop back in the basin we had planned for them later in the week. This group of mostly college students dealt with a week of hail, clogged water purifiers, scanty and often impossible-to-follow trails, and the shortage of three days' worth of supplies. To this day, most of those students will tell anyone who will listen to their tales of difficulty and suffering that it was one of the greatest weeks of their lives!

I know it was partially my own lack of a weighty life that led to my undoing late in 2009. Recently, I spent a few months talking through life with a counselor and friend of mine in Denver who helped me see my own life as largely one-dimensional. The result for me was a lightness that kept me from landing in solid presence in my own context and embracing existence in all its complexity—perhaps even appreciating the hard, scratchy things in my midst. Throughout our weeks together, Bob would often ask me how I felt, specifically what my body was telling me. Inevitably, I would point directly to the base of my sternum, where a constant pain had developed, a sick and nauseating physical pain my body had produced in response to my emotional fear. At the time, I felt this like a weight I continually carried in my chest.

I would like to delve into this more in the section on fear, but for now, I want to focus on an afternoon event that I believe demonstrates what it means to begin to acquire weight. It was becoming clear to me by this point that my life was largely one-dimensional. I had learned to live my life from the realm of the mind, compensating for the lack of a soul and emotional life by reasoning and thinking more. Like many of the ghosts in Lewis's *Great Divorce*, I may have appeared as an individual of substance, being appointed to oversee church-planting efforts over a five-state region at age thirty-three, but I was essentially hollow at the core and light enough that the grass of heaven would have hurt my feet. Though overactive and able to sustain for almost forty years, my mind could not compensate for the lack of a fully integrated life; it simply did not carry enough weight to ground me in existence.

As this reality began to take hold and I acknowledged the fear that had caused me to live from only part of my life, something dramatic occurred. As Bob and I talked one day, I had the surprising and very real sensation that something significant was happening in the hollow place in my sternum where only nausea and pain had been present for over a year. As a means of describing the event, try to picture a large steel ball bearing being deposited in the center of this very spot. It was a very real image of something large and heavy with substance placed in the core of my being. As Bob watched this occur, he said to me, "That's your soul." I hope to clarify this image somewhat as we discuss fear and integration in subsequent sections. For now, suffice it to say, what I realized was that the pain and weight my chaotic life had been producing the previous year was not really a weight at all but a cloud, a dark cloud with only the ability to darken and obscure. As this ephemeral cloud continues to arise from time to time now, it is quickly shown for what it is. The cloud cannot move the solid core but only obscure it momentarily or dissipate on meeting it.

So begins a period of life where I am learning to acquire weight and to approach all the rough, hot, cold, scratchy, uncomfortable things of my context. For the first time in life, I am able to more fully understand and appreciate why I am drawn so inexorably to the wild places of the mountains and the deserts. These hard experiences help us to acquire self-knowledge, integration, and a weighty existence. I believe this solid bearinglike core is the reality of a soul that allows me to engage the hard elements of emotional interaction. The multifaceted complexity of life, the importance of fear, and a desire to be integrated are all parts of the important cycle to cultivating an existence of weight—something we desperately need in order to make a life in our twenty-first century.

Published in 1984, *The Unbearable Lightness of Being* by Czechoslovakian Milan Kundera has been called the quintessential postmodern novel. The book is set in Prague in 1968 and particularly focusses on the August 1968 invasion by the Soviet Union. The story is primarily about Thomas, a womanizing surgeon and intellectual, and Tereza, a young woman from a small Czech town who becomes Thomas's wife and takes up photography after she moves to Prague. The historical setting in which the characters find themselves and the development of the approaches to life they embody are lucid illustrations of lives of lightness and weight.

Thomas seems to have the life so many aim for. He is handsome and unattached, and he's a professional in his field with a large income. His situation allows him to pursue life as he sees fit, which he does through trysts with multiple women. The surprise appearance of Tereza at his doorstep following a chance encounter throws Thomas's life into turmoil—he is soon forced into a position where he has to question his life of unattached lightness. Kundera contrasts the light and free life of Thomas with the seriousness and weight with which Tereza lives. She soon takes up photography and finds herself particularly interested in chronicling the circumstances surrounding the Soviet occupation of Prague. Thomas and Tereza are soon exiled to Zurich, where she suffers loneliness for her own people while Thomas, oblivious to anyone else's struggle with life, continues his lifestyle of utter abandonment. Tereza, with her weighty life still intact, must return to the war-torn people of Czechoslovakia. The end of the novel finds the pair living a relatively quiet life in the countryside.

The contrast and lessons Kundera brings to mind are profound. To be utterly isolated from the plight of those in one's own community and pursue only personal pleasure and profession make up the unbearable lightness of being in the end. Tereza ends up being a sort of savior for Thomas because of the proximity he is able to have to one with weight. Tereza is not only entirely faithful to Thomas even in light of his escapades, but she is at the same time engaged in the suffering and situations of those in her world. Like Lewis before him, Kundera paints a picture rich with implications for endeavoring to find a rich and meaningful life. The consummate advertising in our culture elevates consumption, reputation, and sexual prowess as the keys to a fulfilled life—things that perpetuate a lightness of being in their tendency to distract us from the hard things of life, which ultimately give us substance, meaning, and weight. The issue of our penchant for the light over and above the heavy is one of the causes of our confusion when we fail to find life as enjoyable as others promised it would be. We somehow have to reengage the rough, hot, cold, scratchy, uncomfortable things.

One crucial way I am learning to cultivate this addition of weight to life is through wild trips to wild places. Zac and I often purposefully choose harder approaches to the peaks we climb, steering clear of more leisurely routes. Perhaps it was largely unconscious at first, but as the difficulty of a trip increases—because of a longer approach over a broken ridge or a climb attempted in deep winter—we found our enjoyment increasing, and these trips become far more memorable. I don't want to misrepresent our abilities or strength of character. As with any "weighty" experience in life, the enjoyment often fails to come until hours or in some cases, days after the trip. Fear and difficulty inevitably add weight and significance to such endeavors. In *Desert Solitaire*, Ed Abbey quips, "All things excellent are as difficult as they are rare, said a wise man. If so, what happens to excellence when we eliminate the difficulty and the rarity" (Abbey, 1968)?

So we choose to climb La Plata Peak via the treacherous two-mile-long, class-three Elingwood Ridge rather than take the easier and shorter Northwest Ridge. We choose to summit Mount of the Holy Cross via the snow-covered Holy Cross Couloir rather than take the walk-up utilizing the North Ridge. We utilized a break from class and work over President's Day for years to repeatedly climb (at times attempt to climb) Little Bear Peak, a difficult climb even in summer months. The pursuit of the difficult and weighty led me to a solo attempt on Gannett Peak's west side via the Minor Glacier one summer rather than the well-traveled Glacier Trail approach. I recall on one particularly difficult outing, most likely off route again on Mt. Wilson's East Face, attempting to introduce some levity into our situation by somewhat rhetorically asking Zac, "Isn't this great?"

He replied, "You know better than that. Ask me two hours after we're off." The situations that add weight to life are often not all that "great" when we find ourselves in their midst. It is not until the following days and years that we recognize what these have added to our lives and they take on their full significance.

In October one year, my son, William, and I headed into the Grand Gulch of southern Utah for three days backpacking together. We utilized the access point at Collins Canyon to reach the Wetherill Trail in the bottom of the gulch, which we followed to the unusual Bannister House Ruin perched high on the cliff wall. We also had plans to visit the expansive Red, White, and Blue Panel of pictographs, which potentially entailed backtracking many miles past Collins Canyon. After we studied our topographic map, we agreed instead on a bolder plan—a nearly one-thousand-foot vertical ascent out of the trailless Deer Canyon, an open crossing of Polly Mesa, and a reentry into the Grand Gulch via the many armed Water Canyon. This would entail many miles of trailless, open ground and climbing in and out of canyons neither of us had seen before.

Early on our second day, we began our climb out of Deer Canyon, almost continually expecting to round each corner of the canyon and find ourselves in the shadow of an impassable dry-fall. We were able to find a way onto Polly Mesa, and then we followed some landmarks to the head of Water Canyon. Water Canyon, like many such cuts into the topography of the southwest desert, is actually a series of narrow canyons sunk deep into the rock of the Cedar Mesa Sandstone with many pour-offs and dry-falls barring the way into upper or lower reaches. Willy and I made our way into a promising canyon only to be stopped at its lower end by a hundred-foot fall. We were forced to climb back out of the canyon and cross into the next tributary to the south to try our luck again. This short canyon had its own pour-off into the main fork of Water Canyon, but William and I found if we moved very carefully to skirt the fall on one side, then we might find a way in. We finally reached the main tributary of the Grand Gulch just before dark and collapsed into our bags following a quick supper. To this day, I am convinced that the ruins and pictographs of the lower Grand Gulch hold special prominence in our minds precisely because of the effort we extended to view them. One of my most valuable possessions to this day is a picture of William sitting below Bannister House Ruin.

How would an individual move beyond the unbearable lightness many of us spend a lifetime cultivating? We could begin by choosing to immerse ourselves in the real situations of our world, particularly of our neighborhood, rather than feigning fatigue after a "hard day" and insulating ourselves behind the entertainment of 150 channels. We could begin by engaging in the hard, hot, cold, scratchy, often uncomfortable nature of relationships rather than bailing out the first chance we get. Some of us could begin interacting with and perhaps disciplining our children rather than abandoning them to the values of advertising and consumption. Perhaps for someone to cultivate the weightiness in life, that person must quit his or her job—or perhaps the person will need keep his or her job! Others will need to battle their self-indulgence by sticking to diets or exercise regimes beyond the discomfort of the first three months.

I know what I would do. I would schedule a wild trip to a wild place that scares me to death. Bob often reminded me that to have weight and substance is to land solidly in the world with presence. You have to actually show up emotionally to the experience of life to learn to love where you are. Without weight, we are like the inhabitants of the quarantined city in Albert Camus's book *The Plague*, trapped in a life without meaning, hope, or escape. "Thus, in a middle course between these heights and depths, they drifted through life rather than lived, the prey of aimless days and sterile moments, like wandering shadows that could have acquired substance only by consenting to root themselves in the solid earth of their distress." Camus has two of his principle characters share this dialogue:

> "One has the idea that [humanity] is capable of everything."

> "I can't agree; he is incapable of suffering for a long time, or being happy for a long time. Which means that he's incapable of anything really worthwhile." (Camus, 1972)

Granted, the concept of a life "heavy" with the engagement of our world and its inhabitants is not easy for most of us to swallow. To consider actually opening our emotional life to the reality and plight of the context we inhabit is more than many of us can stomach, so we tend to return to the bus time and again in order to escape a land with substance—just as the characters in *The Great Divorce*. We tend to excuse our lack of involvement or engagement with excuses of busyness, fatigue, and stress. An honest examination, however, reveals that these elements of our lives are most often born in contexts designed to keep us moving through life as light as possible: our jobs, purchases, and even "busyness" doing relatively little other than spinning our wheels. The trade-off in our failing to make decisions to acquire weight is a "flat" existence whereby even our ability to experience joy is stilted. As we diminish our interest in the weighty things of existence, so we diminish our ability to look honestly at our pedestrian lives as well as experience any real passion for the things of life we once thought would please us so much. Like failing to grasp life in its complexity, this flatness has become unbearable for so many that their hearts and lives have been given to addiction or they have simply closed themselves off to any real consideration about wherein life might be found or recovered.

In his classic work, *Pensées*, Blaise Pascal says that man's condition consists of inconstancy, boredom and anxiety. "The basis of all this lies in the wretchedness of human existence. Realizing this, they have taken to diversions ... take away their diversions and you will see them bored to extinction. Then they feel their nullity without recognizing it, for nothing could be more wretched than to be intolerably depressed as soon as one is reduced to introspection with no means of diversion" (Pascal, 1970). To acquire weight would force us to deal with life apart from our diversions of consumption, careerism, and addiction.

Pascal makes the point that the only constant thing about humanity is its desire to be happy. In order to be happy, one must not think about the self, our condition, or our finitude because to be alone with such thoughts would only make us unhappy. The result is the plethora of diversions we fill our lives with that actually have no meaning despite our attempts to convince ourselves otherwise. In reality, our diversions are aimed at distracting us because of the unbearable lightness of our being. It is our flat existence that cannot experience the height of real joy or love because it does not have the substantive capacity to do so. We would be far less apt to be so afraid of ourselves or our condition if we were to acquire a weight and substance in the soul—a substance which we could learn to be comfortable to be with because we found it rich and heavy with meaning.

To live a life of weight is to cultivate a renewed passion for life and our world, one that is not the empty passion of chaos and fleeting pleasure but an appreciation full of real emotion. Most of us experienced this state as children when even the smallest thing could hold hours of enjoyment and we weren't afraid to be exceedingly happy or even distraught. Somewhere, most of us learned how to guard our inner lives closely, and we lost the corresponding capacity to actually enjoy. John Muir wrote, "Most people are on the world, not in it—have no conscious sympathy or relationship to anything about them—undiffused, separate, and rightly alone like marbles of polished stone, touching but separate" (Teale, 2001). Muir's answer was found in a life bathed in the wild places of the Sierras of California.

———

I am inclined to believe that in some sense the concept of weight is at least partially behind the life of Everett Ruess, who disappeared into the southern Utah desert wilderness in 1934 at the age of twenty-one. Many have doubtlessly read Ruess's life story as a tragedy and extravagant waste, but it stands in sharp contrast to the unbearable lightness of being so many of us cultivate in our postmodern context. Ruess was an accomplished student from a good family in California when he began wandering the wild places of California, Arizona, Nevada, Utah, and Colorado at the age of sixteen. He eventually began to spend longer and longer periods in these isolated and secluded settings until he mysteriously disappeared in the Escalante region of Utah. In the introduction to *A Vagabond for Beauty*, a combination of reflections on his life and a collection of letters he had sent home during his travels, the author of the introduction, John Nichols, writes, "His determination to plod alone through the Southwestern wilderness was so fierce and arrogant that at times he seemed to be utterly consumed … It is not that the man took leave of his senses, but rather that he was totally enflamed by a wonderful awareness of them." Nichols reflects that to Ruess "his life must have seemed incredibly whole as he wandered over the land" (Rusho, 2002).

The point is not for all of us to throw off all of life and responsibility to simply escape to the wilderness but rather to recognize the lesson of a life full of weight because it had been in touch with deep passion and emotion and appreciation, a life fully grounded and set down in the present. "Today, for the most part, we have lost the capacity for wonder which so moved [F. Scott] Fitzgerald, and which drove Everett toward the fascinating doom he yearned to embrace" (Rusho, 2002).

Ruess wrote a letter to his brother Waldo in which he explains, "I have had some terrific experiences in the wilderness since I wrote to you—overpowering, overwhelming. But then I am always being overwhelmed. I require it to sustain life." Far from wanting the diversion from the human condition and the brevity of life, Ruess wrote about wanting to embrace the weighty significance of life as it stood. "Finality does not appall me and I seem to always enjoy things more intensely because of the certainty that they will not last." He admitted that a reason for being so unrestrained was that "always I sense the brink of things." This brief life in some ways illustrates being immersed in the hot, cold, hard, scratchy things of life, which grants us a weight to root ourselves in the solid world, the weight with which we can actually be present to the beauty and even tragedy of creation. Nichols concludes, "The message every poet and vagabond seeker like Ruess leaves behind is simple: Life on the earth is very precious and very beautiful" (Rusho, 2002).

I quoted Sigurd Olson earlier: "There is a penalty for too much comfort and ease, a penalty of lassitude and inertia and the frustrated feeling that comes with unreality." Sojourns into wild places, even if brief, have the capacity to take us out of our comfort zones, away from our diversions, and into a context where we can begin to appreciate the value of acquiring substance even through privation and suffering for discovering a vital portion of life. "I cannot abide the thought of a flat existence. Some self-knowledge is all that we can hope for from life, and it is no small thing. Whatever small measure of it I've accumulated has come from the mountains" (Crouch, 2002). Doubtless for most of us, to begin to accept weight we'll first have to deal with fear.

3

FEAR

It must be poor life that achieves freedom from fear.
—*ALDO LEOPOLD*

IN THE MONTHS following the avalanche on Colorado's Quandry Peak, I found myself attempting to again make my way up high peaks on snowy slopes. Most often that first summer, I would retreat after a short distance on a steep grade, always feeling that the slope under my feet would come off the mountain with the next step. I spent most of the summer of 2005 believing that I would never again find the nerve to actually summit a mountain, though I continued to try. Finally in October of that year, bolstered by the presence of my long-time climbing partner Zac, we were determined to make a go of it again. We chose as our destination a high point in the Indian Peaks of Colorado just west of Denver. We spent most of the day driving from Omaha, and after a few miles of trail approach in the evening, we set a camp in a high basin just south of our target.

Early the following morning, Zac and I traveled a well-used trail as it followed switchbacks up broad slopes to a high saddle at nearly thirteen thousand feet on the peak's east side. At this point, we made an important choice. Instead of following the easier East Ridge to the summit, which essentially amounted to a walk-up, we descended almost a thousand feet into a large basin on the peak's north side from which we hoped to ascend a large glacier to the summit. As the glaciated north face began to steepen, Zac and I strapped on our crampons and took ice axes in hand to slowly kick our way to the summit. Even today, years later, I can pause to consider that fall afternoon and the fear which rose in my stomach that day in 2005 is as palpable as if I were on the mountain today. The higher I ascended, the more ominous the mountain seemed to become. Each step seemed to sink deeper into the slope as if I were about to break the entire glacier off the massif by my presence. Sounds of cracking and settling and sloughing became constant and louder with each foot of ascent. I found myself attempting to move unusually quickly as I climbed, as if by mere speed, I could get off this slope and avoid bringing another mountain down on top of me. Only a few times in my life has relief been as immediate and welcome as when I reached the rock-lined summit ridge a few yards from the peak. I had spent hours that day fully immersed in the throes of tangible fear.

On our easier descent of the East Ridge that afternoon, I discovered that Zac had spent his climb in a deep conversation with his own fear much like I had with mine. A couple of years before this climb, Zac and I were on the Emperor Couloir on Torrey Peak during our annual Christmas climb. Torrey Peak is considered a "Front Range" peak, and the Emperor Couloir rises three thousand feet from its base, making it one of the longest snow climbs in

Colorado. After he had summited Torrey that December, Zac was making his way across a narrow ridge when the overhanging cornice he was on collapsed and sent Zac careening down the steep and hardened upper slopes of the couloir. He began sliding uncontrollably down hundreds of feet of frozen snow, gaining speed, pointed directly toward an ominous boulder field far below. It is important to note that Zac is an accomplished mountaineer and well-practiced in self-arrest. But in an uncontrolled fall when one's ice axe is flailing wildly from the leash on the wrist, rolling over on the head of the axe is not always possible. It was likely the sheer mercy of God that stopped Zac's rapid descent just a few feet before he would have careened wildly over the exposed boulder field. As he came to rest and lay back in the snow out of sheer relief, some of the debris kicked loose from the fall rolled directly onto the top of Zac's head. When I and other climbers in our party reached Zac soon afterward, we found that he had a dislocated shoulder and that blood was running off of his head down the side of his face. This kind of experience makes an indelible impression on a climber for years.

As we made our way off the Indian Peak summit, I shared with Zac how I had spent the day climbing as quickly as my legs and lungs would allow simply to be free of the slope that I was sure would slough off any moment. Zac told me that the thought had never crossed his mind. The snow was solid, and the conditions were perfect for a climb that day. Instead, he had spent his day fearing that with each step, he would lose purchase and go sliding into the gaping crevasse at the bottom of the slope. I, on the other hand, had never considered that a possibility as I felt sure-footed with the bite of my axe and ten-point crampons. We each summited that October day, fighting through our own separate fears created by experiences from our pasts.

I wish I could say that in the last five years, I have learned to put my fear behind me and climb free from the thoughts that plagued me in the months following the avalanche, but that would simply be disingenuous. I'm not sure I can identify a slope I have been on that I didn't feel could simply disconnect from a mountain and cascade to the bottom with me somewhere in the middle. To some degree, I have simply learned to continue to climb with fear as my constant companion. At the same time, I am not convinced this is an entirely negative experience as I approach the mountains now with a greater respect and humility than I did before my experiences. Fear can indeed be a teacher, and it is often an important partner in risky endeavors. What does continue to surprise me, however, is how I learned to live with and even court my fear in the outdoors long before I learned how to do this with the rest of life. Acknowledging and even embracing fear, like the realities of complexity and weight, would doubtlessly have saved me a great deal of personal darkness.

It is helpful to understand some of the physiology of fear in order to recognize what it does to our lives on a regular basis. Fear is an emotional response that forms part of a larger system in our bodies. It is designed to work quickly and powerfully motivate behavior. Emotion is largely instructive and aimed at the self-preservation of a species. We all recognize the automatic responses of emotional instinct: the smile at joy, tears at grief, a physically startled reaction at a surprising noise or a person in the dark. Writing about the way emotion tends to dominate the functions of the whole body Laurence Gonzales says, "[Emotion] involves numerous bodily changes that are preparations for action. The nervous system fires more rapidly, the blood changes its chemistry so that it can coagulate more rapidly, muscle tone alters, digestion stops, and various chemicals flood the body to put it in a state of high readiness for whatever needs done. All of that happens outside of conscious control. Reason is tentative, slow, and fallible, while emotion is sure, quick and unhesitating" (Gonzales, 2003).

Emotions, particularly fear, activate the mind and work on the body in complex ways. Scientists have discovered two pathways by which stimuli enter the brain. One is through the neocortex, which tends to process information on a cognitive level, helping us recognize what we see or taste for example. Stimuli travels through another quicker pathway (even if by a few milliseconds) by means of the amygdala, which serves as a sort of watchdog screening information for signs of danger. "So information from the senses takes a neural route that splits, one part reaching the amygdala first, the other arriving at the neocortex milliseconds later. Rational (or conscious) thought always lags behind emotional reaction" (Gonzales, 2003). If the amygdala senses a dangerous situation, it immediately releases a flow of multiple chemicals into the body from the adrenal glands (the familiar so-called "adrenaline rush"), which causes the heart rate to rise and breathing rate to increase. Sugar is dumped into the metabolic system, and oxygen and nutrients are shifted to areas of the body that may be necessary to run or fight. Fear is a powerful force on our body precisely because it is automatic. We react in ways we can't always control and often don't even think about these reactions. Emotional responses occur in our bodies immediately, often before we can engage reason to convince us that we should respond otherwise. In his study on the concept of the "sublime," Edmund Burke wrote as early as the mid-eighteenth century, "Whatever is fitted in any sort to excite the ideas of pain, and danger, that is to say, whatever is in any sort terrible, or is conversant about terrible objects, or operates in a manner analogous to terror, is a sense of the sublime; that is, it is productive of the strongest emotion which the mind is capable of feeling" (Burke, 1757).

The science behind reactions like fear partially explains why it is so powerful in our lives. It tends to express itself in very physical ways, and the chemicals dictate activity in ways we would not tend to engage in if left purely to reason. I spent nearly two years reading gas and electric meters for an energy company in southern Colorado. The job put me in countless alleys and backyards on a monthly basis. One summer afternoon, I was approaching the backyard of a home through an alley when I spied a pit bull chained on a mound in a large area between the alley and backyard fence. I had passed this particular dog on numerous occasions, but I remember that afternoon actually thinking that the pit bull could break his chain whenever he wanted to, which happened to occur on that day. Apparently, the dog knew the limits of his chain because as he sprinted toward me, he seemed to strain at precisely the right moment. Suddenly, he was free to have his way with me. I didn't have any consciously stored-up skills to guide me in an actual "dogfight," but I instinctively lowered my body to squat at his level while I swung my handheld computer to strike a blow on his left jaw. My intention was to back the dog away long enough so I could reach down with my left hand and collect a handful of rocks that dogs were averse to having hurled at them.

It was the aftermath of the encounter that most surprised me. After the immediate danger, when the pit bull was finally backed down, it was as if the adrenaline spike in my system had to be dealt with. I found myself reaching for a solid, discarded bowling pin that was lying nearby and actually giving chase to the dog through other yards. My fear had given way to fierce anger. I had heard similar accounts from my good friend Dave, who was a twenty-year veteran of reading meters in this region. Dave is an accomplished artist and has a gentle soul full of deep compassion. On one occasion, however, he had been relentlessly pursued through a neighborhood by a Rottweiler. He fled over fences, across streets, and through numerous yards. When Dave finally reached his work truck, he found his fear turning to anger as he procured an iron pipe and proceeded to turn on his attacker, chasing the dog wildly down the street while hurling many choice words through an otherwise quiet neighborhood. Fear can act on even the gentlest soul in very surprising and vivid ways. It tends to dominate an otherwise sane, reasoning mind.

The very real rush that fear brings to the surface likely lies behind the rising popularity of extreme sports and so-called adrenaline junkies, activities that help many individuals feel something viscerally in their bodies. I headed to the Utah desert one morning, planning to descend Larry Canyon by myself, a technical slot canyon in the Robber's Roost area. I happened to meet four young men from Jackson, Wyoming, who were dropping a shuttle vehicle for the same canyon. I was graciously invited to join the group and happily did so. Tied into the rope at the top of the second rappel, I said out loud, though more to myself than anyone, "I'm actually afraid of heights." The most skilled and accomplished climber of the group was close enough to hear and responded, "So am I. That's why I climb." There is definitely something rather life-affirming that surfaces in the body and emotions when we can learn to court our fears in environments where at least some of the risk and danger can be mitigated (through the use of ropes, for instance) while the place still retains enough of the unknown to allow strong emotions to produce a physical response.

Despite the growth in crowds of people flocking to engage in risky activity, fear on a more internal level is not something we have learned to deal with very well. The circumstances that produce emotional fear (as opposed to physical fear, which may seem like an anomaly) cannot always be mitigated or so well controlled by us so as to remove as much risk. We don't typically appreciate fear in our contemporary context precisely because it seems so primitive—an unthinking, automatic response we have a hard time controlling. Fear is not subject to the thinking mind we depend on so much to engineer and control our circumstances. For Joseph Conrad, the boat ride up river into the wilderness details a journey past the civilized engineering of life into the depths of primitive emotional responses we have largely lost the capacity to deal with.

> Land in a swamp, march through the woods, and in some inland post feel the savagery, the utter savagery, has closed round him—all that mysterious life of the wilderness that settles in the forest, in the jungles, in the hearts of wild men. There's no initiation, either, into such mysteries. He has to live in the midst of the incomprehensible, which is also detestable. And it has a fascination, too, that goes to work on him. The fascination of the abomination. (Conrad, 1910)

In order to understand what this discussion of fear has to do with learning to respond rightly to life and building a healthy, complex existence, we need to take what we've learned thus far and make the transition to the fears prevalent in our emotional lives. Consider, for example, the emotional fear produced in a jilted lover. The experience is one of rejection which may come from being left or abandoned by a spouse, a close friend, or one's parents. Because fear has self-preservation as its aim, the fear created when one is rejected often produces an automatic response that reason alone probably wouldn't produce. Self-protective measures are often employed, which may cause an individual to refuse to become emotionally invested or avoid the experience of pain through compensating behaviors, perhaps with drugs or consumptive addictions. Because of the way fear surfaces in the subconscious, it creates a stronger memory pattern for the mind. Individuals often find life locked into patterns of behavior that are merely instruments for dealing with the unconscious presence of fear in the emotional life.

As with an encounter with an attacking dog, fear can give way to anger. Angry responses and actions are often the result of someone pushing an individual into an emotional corner so that his or her fear becomes present—whether that fear is something acknowledged or not. We see this behavior in violent, angry youth or continuously pissed-off elderly people who may not understand what they're so disgruntled about. Because fear as an emotion often bypasses the cognitive centers of the mind, it can produce patterns in us that we never set out to create for ourselves and probably have a hard time understanding. Not knowing (or being able to know because of our subconscious natures) how to control fear as a means of self-preservation will eventually lead many to a basic denial of its consummate reality. We avoid acknowledging it because it implies our lack of ability to control and order our circumstances.

I sat in Bob's office one afternoon when I was confronted with a simple question: "What are you afraid of?" I'm not sure if Bob asked me this out of frustration with my lack of forward movement or simply posed it as a means of getting to the heart of things, but its simplicity surprised me. Nothing immediately came to mind, and my initial thought was this: *I work in one of the most dangerous industries in the world and climb ice mountains on the weekends for fun. I'm not afraid of anything.* Apparently, Bob knew better and simply met my lack of engagement with patient silence. One of the most remarkable moments of my life soon followed. I know what fear feels like. As a novice climber who also happens to be afraid of heights, I have often put myself in positions where fear is very palpable. The experience is akin to vertigo. A common dictionary definition of vertigo is "a sensation of motion in which the individual or the individual's surroundings seem to whirl dizzily." Often on a high, exposed ridge or on a steep snow face or at the head of a long rappel into a dark, narrow slot the earth around me can feel as if it's moving. Despite the fact that I'm standing perfectly still, it seems as if I am moving, swaying dizzily and already in the throes of a fall.

Fearful situations like these put knots in the stomach and adrenaline in the throat. We often begin to sweat as blood rushes to the surface of the skin in preparation for action. Now all of these physical sensations were beginning to manifest themselves from the comfortable environs of a counselor's office. It was quickly apparent that I was afraid! Approaching the reality and constant presence of fear in my life, which had automatically produced a protected way of life for me for more than thirty years, had produced all of the physical manifestations of the emotion with which I was very familiar. It was as if I had walked up to the edge of what was frustrating my life and peeked into a gaping abyss. For some reason, Nietzsche's words came to mind. "Look not long into the abyss lest the abyss look into you." I was standing at the edge of a precipice, gazing off into dark depths, and I immediately recoiled at the fear.

This is not an experience entirely unfamiliar to those who spend much time in the outdoors. Whether one is climbing on a high, exposed mountain slope, trekking the isolated north woods of the Alaskan frontier, or traversing in a barren desert environment, one often comes face-to-face with some kind of "abyss." Writing in his *Nature's Kindred Spirits*, James McClintock points out that in Jack London's stories "the solitary figure in the landscape is brought to the edge of the abyss, at which point he is either broken or discovers a link with life beyond anything that can be imagined in civilization. Similarly, [Edward] Abbey's works ... are haunted by the threat of despair met by questing until one stares into the abyss and comes to terms with life. Remember, for instance, the passage from 'Coda: Cape Solitude' in which Abbey literally stares into an isolated canyon abyss and has despair altered to 'a roaring affirmation of existence'" (McClintock, 1994). Looking into the dark depths of an abyss, which is often no further away than one's soul, should be a familiar experience for one often alone in the wilderness.

I wish I could write that I pressed into the fear as I have often found myself doing on a difficult climb. I wish I could claim that the physical manifestations of my fear produced the fight response in me, whereby I rose up to walk into the abyss. Instead, I regained control of my emotions, calmed myself down, and fled like a small child from the monster in the closet.

For a year, I fled at full speed into self-destruction, avoiding the acknowledgment of the fear, which was always present and had created self-preserving patterns in my life. It was as if I could deny this thing and hide my emotional fears from the rest of my existence indefinitely.

Fortunately, I had seen too much and knew too much about fear to put off the reality forever. Not long after that afternoon in Bob's office, Zac forwarded me a photo he had snapped a couple of years before of me rappelling off the first drop into Alcatraz Canyon in Utah. Alcatraz begins with a nearly 180-foot free rappel anchored from the bumper of one's vehicle. Zac captioned the picture, "You can't be *that* afraid of heights." Months later, with no emotional life or resources left, it was as if I had no choice but to reengage the process of dealing with my fear. I found myself again in the not-so-safe but imminently friendly confines of Bob's office where the reality of my fear came to me in an instant. Despite being forty years old, I was afraid I didn't really belong to the world of men.

My father had left home when I was about fifteen years old, so I had missed a great deal of a dad's affirmation and initiation into the world of men. I spent many years as an emotional child, doing what I could to earn the approval and place in a man's world. For me, this manifested itself in a life of ascendency and expertise gained through knowledge and hard work. I was something of an athlete, serving as captain of my high school and college football teams. I was a good student earning good grades and scholarships and graduating with a master's degree in historical theology. I taught and spoke regularly to groups as an "expert" having answers to the life of the soul. At only thirty-three, I was appointed as a director of church-planting over five states. Even after I left the church and worked in the oil field, I was made a driller over a rig with a five-man crew in only ten months. I married well and was raising three healthy, beautiful, and talented children. But at the end of the day, all of my activity was largely a response to fear: I thought that at some point, I would be revealed as a pretender in this world. I couldn't stay in any given context for long, lest someone recognize that I didn't know as much as I let on. I feared I didn't measure up, and the fear had created automatic, compensating patterns in my life.

My dad was a great man with the qualities of an excellent father. He provided well for his family. He was strong and quiet with an excellent work ethic. He rarely lost his temper, and he was never given to violence. At the same time, I believe that my dad was likely dealing with his own unacknowledged fears, many of which kept him in silent desperation. He and my mother were married and became parents when they were both very young. Dad was haunted by the death of his sixteen-year-old sister, who had been killed in a car accident while she was left in his care. For years, there was very little income in our household of five. Many years later, I can sympathize with the circumstances that manifested themselves in my father's incapacity to be emotionally engaged with me as a small child. But at the time, my young mind translated silence as a judgment on my value. I thought I really wasn't worth all that much. The lack of physical touch and emotional affirmation left a young boy deeming himself as somehow worthless. I don't believe the fault was so much my dad's as I refuse to believe he would actually say something like that; the fault lies in my own unhealthy attachment to my own ways of compensating for fear.

We know that fear as an emotion is aimed at self-preservation. The fear of being worthless and not really belonging in the world in any significant way can encourage acts of compensation in order for us to somehow preserve a will to keep going. For many, the response is one of addiction. For others it is ascendency. Regardless, it comes as a mostly automatic, unacknowledged, patterned response to the subconscious emotional presence of fear. My own life then became a series of judgments. I thought that I should be somewhere else, doing something else with someone else because whatever I had could not possibly be construed as worthwhile. These patterned responses to life would have doubtlessly gone on indefinitely had I not come to a place where I could acknowledge fear and learn to do something constructive with it. In some regard, fear can actually serve as an important teacher.

This is one important reason why for me sojourning in wild places has become so critical. As I learn to integrate life and lay the lessons of the wilderness over my context, I see what we can learn from acknowledging fear. Fear is not necessarily the thing to be avoided, but we should try to limit our unhealthy responses to the fears we harbor. In his own chronicles of a climbing life and the lessons it holds for existing as a human in our current context, Gregory Crouch writes,

> Ironically, those are precisely the moments I try constantly to avoid. If I were more of a man I'd say: 'Give me the wild, insecure moments when fear has the bile up in my throat, when desire sits like a lead weight in my gut, and when the summit is maybe, just maybe, within reach.' But I don't have the courage to ask for

those moments. Each time up I hope, I beg, for an easy climb. I hope to climb and descend without hassle, without fear, without storm. But I know that I am the best man I can ever hope to be precisely in those moments of maximum fear and doubt. (Crouch, 2002)

In *The Great Divorce*, C. S. Lewis paints a scene that masterfully illustrates how fear is not really the issue. Instead, the issue lies in what our fear attempts to cover in our lives through so many automatic, patterned responses. The narrator comes across one of the ghostly figures from earth that happens to have a red lizard on his shoulder, a reptile that is constantly whispering things in the ghost's ear. The lizard immediately struck me as a picture of the sense of worthlessness I carried for years; however, it could equally stand as one's insecurity, inadequacy, or abandonment. What's interesting is how the lizard continuously whispers in his host's ear, and the ghost is alternately angered and comforted by the words. Many of us may be appalled at our lack of "getting things together," and yet we often find the only comforts we have in these self-protective measures are the ones we've built up through a lifetime of responding only out of fear. The ghost is then approached by an angelic figure who promises freedom from the lizard, but only if the man can kill it. An interesting dialogue follows in which the lizard's host finds many excuses for putting off the demise of the whispering presence—one of which is his conviction that killing the lizard would mean killing the self. We find the following exchange between the ghost and his angelic teacher.

[Ghost] "Get back! You're hurting me. How can I tell you to kill it? You'd kill me if you did."

[Angel] "It is not so."

[Ghost] "Why, you're hurting me now."

[Angel] "I never said it wouldn't hurt you. I said it wouldn't kill you."

The lizard itself then begins to chime in with its own defense for leaving things as they are as it chatters to the ghost it rides on. "He can kill me. One fatal word from you and he will! Then you'll be without me forever and ever. It's not natural. How could you live? You'd be only a sort of ghost, not a real man as you are now. ... Yes, yes, I know there are no real pleasures, now, only dreams. But aren't they better than nothing?"

"Have I your permission?" said the angel to the ghost.

"I know it will kill me."

"It won't. But supposing it did?"

"You're right. It would be better to be dead than to live with this creature." (Lewis, 1946)

The ghost does concede to the killing of the lizard, and what ensues is the transformation of a figure of unbearable lightness into a solid substance of a man of gold. Even the lizard itself is transfigured into a stallion on which the new being rides off toward a mountain. Lewis is a master of the metaphor. We realize that fear sets up a series of subconscious, lifelong responses that at some point we believe we could never live without because we cannot remember life before the fear and because these responses were birthed in us out of what our emotional lives felt were self-preservation moments. There may not be much in the way of real and fulfilled life—only dreams—but we tell ourselves that these are better than nothing.

What we also see in the story is that fear, rightly recognized and walked into, can actually serve us. Fear can serve as a gateway into what it is that is keeping our lives stuck in lightness, disharmony, or disillusion. Vertigo sets in as soon as we ask honestly, "What am I afraid of?" and our whole world begins to reel and pitch despite the fact that we're standing still. An encounter like this can feel like death because of the strength of accumulated memories and unconscious responses that might feel like stronger instincts than conscious thought. We can feel at these moments as if we're falling and falling to our very death. I have experienced major and traumatic falls, but fear itself is not the thing that will kill us. Fear acknowledged can serve as the thing that we use to ride into the very heart of what keeps our lives frustrated and never really present to the weight and complexity of the world in our midst. It is important for us to find a safe place and safe people of substance with which to encounter our fear so that we might press through it to the circumstances that cause us to live the half-lives so many of us have settled for.

I have long believed that the deserts and mountains provide a context of privation and insecurity, one that helps us court fear enough to know we can walk through it and emerge as healthier individuals. Wild places with wild animals and wild weather have drawn seekers out of the small confines of their lives for centuries. Until we can learn to recognize and walk through episodes of fear, our lives will likely continue to be spent in flight—flight from difficult relationships or jobs or circumstances—as a means of self-preservation. Apart from believing in the worthwhile nature of fear, we will continue to attempt to order life or allow it to disintegrate into chaos. We will miss those things that could add weight and substance to our existence.

Laurence Gonzales has spent years studying disasters and dangerous situations and exploring why some people survive while others perish. He has collected many of his conclusions in a book titled *Deep Survival*. Early on, Gonzales begins to talk about the reality of fear and its crucial role in survival as he discusses rules for "making it." "The First Rule is: Face reality. Good survivors aren't immune to fear. They know what's happening, and it does 'scare the living shit out of' them. It's all a question of what you do next." He goes on to say rather poignantly, "Fear puts me in my place. It gives me the humility to see things as they are" (Gonzales, 2003). There is good reason why fear has carried over so prominently from human beings' early primitive emotions. It is necessary for our survival. The sooner we acknowledge the presence of fear in our lives, the sooner we can discover what exactly it is we are afraid of and move to address our responses.

⸻

These thoughts were again pressed upon me recently as I made my way into a trailless canyon in the Cedar Mesa region of southern Utah. Cedar Mesa is probably the best place in America to view ancient cliff dwellings of Native Americans in a wild and primitive setting. Homes, storage bins, grinding stones, pottery pieces, and Native artwork have survived the desert environment very well for over eight hundred years. This particular May had been unusually wet and cold for the region, but a dramatic warm-up had occurred just a few days before I was able to get away. The combination of a late, wet spring with a few days of desert heat meant that I was able to enter the desert at the height of its finest season of color as the desert flowers were in full bloom. As I descended into a particularly deep and rugged canyon with no trail or markers, I began to keep my eyes peeled for alcoves on the north wall where ruins were likely to exist. This was my first trip into this particular canyon, and I soon found it difficult to balance my upturned gaze with the task of negotiating thick brush and boulders the size of homes in the canyon bottom. My frustration was compounded by the fact that the upper reaches of the canyon walls were not particularly steep. They tended instead to retreat from the canyon bottom in a series of benches atop boulder-strewn slopes that could not be easily viewed from below. As I descended miles deeper, I remember saying to myself, "I wonder what I'm missing up there."

For years, I have thoroughly enjoyed studying and viewing the culture of "the Ancient Ones" in a primitive and natural setting throughout the Colorado Plateau. I have seen countless ruins, artifacts, and rock-art panels far from the confines of crowds and guided tours. It wasn't long before I had to pause on that beautiful May outing and ask myself about my growing frustration at possibly missing a few more scattered, ancient homes. Throughout the early afternoon, I battled the temptation to climb out of the bottom of the canyon and venture onto one of the horizontal benches in order to gain a better perspective. Such action, however, would have been utterly futile. These benches tend to remain at a consistent elevation while the canyon continues to drop, eventually leaving one "cliffed out," usually far above the canyon floor and most often without any means of safely dropping into the canyon without miles of backtracking. I had other canyons to explore this trip, and I had hoped to utilize this particular drop as an access point to regions elsewhere. As I paused to consider what I was missing, I finally recognized the world right at my feet. The desert was exploding in oranges, blues, purples, yellows, deep maroons, and the bright green of towering cottonwoods. Springs fed cascading pools filled with the songs of the rare desert toad, which had left hundreds of tadpoles swimming in shallow bowls. The fear I harbored that I was missing something was keeping me from fully appreciating the life blossoming all around me. I proceeded down the canyon with a renewed fascination with the life right at my feet. When I returned home later in the week, my camera was filled as never before with the colors of desert flowers … and very few pictures of ancient ruins.

At times, I have thought this plight unique to men sharing my own stage of life, but I am less convinced that this is the case now. Unacknowledged fear causes far too many of us to spend years wondering what we're missing out there, and consequently, we miss the beauty of life right at our feet. Our sense of being unworthy or being unloved or unskilled or unfulfilled creates the fear that we're missing what life really consists of. Many of us create automatic, patterned, lifelong responses to such fear. We witness this in the constant reinvention of images, in abandoned families and jobs, in midlife crises that never seem to do for us what we hope they would, and so the crises end up being perpetual. I don't believe that it is really the fear that is dangerous for us. I believe that it is the failure to see fear as fear and to be able to ask ourselves what is at the root of believing we are missing something else somewhere else out there. Fear can be our servant if we allow it to teach us something about the complexity of life so that our context can begin to weigh on us. Fear is the gateway to our integration.

4

INTEGRATION

> *If the desert is holy, it is because it is a*
> *forgotten place that allows us to remember the*
> *sacred. Perhaps that is why every pilgrimage*
> *to the desert is a pilgrimage to the self. There*
> *is no place to hide and so we are found.*
> —TERRY TEMPEST-WILLIAMS

SOMETHING SIGNIFICANT STIRRED in me the first time I read Edward Abbey's account of his descent into the Maze District of Canyonlands National Park in his now famous *Desert Solitaire*. Of course, in the late 1950s, the region known as "the Maze" was not yet a part of a sprawling national park complex and visits to the region were rare or nonexistent. Abbey and his traveling companion had to track down the only resident in Moab at the time who had claimed to have been in the Maze and then had to negotiate two days of travel on obscure dirt roads built largely by uranium explorations just to get to a point where the Maze could be viewed, let alone entered and explored.

When I read Abbey's account of his decent into the northern section of the area, it immediately struck me as a place I would love to visit. Today, the Maze is a portion of Canyonlands National Park and encompasses hundreds of wild square miles on the west side of the Green and Colorado rivers. Locals often call the region "Under the Ledge," but the Maze is appropriately named as it consists of a wild series of deep canyons forking endlessly into dozens of long tributary canyons often separated by towering cliff escarpments only a few dozen feet wide. When Abbey first camped in this region, he said,

> We can see deep narrow canyons down in there branching out in all directions, and sandy flats with clumps of trees—oaks? cottonwoods? Dividing one canyon from the next are high partitions of nude sandstone, smoothly sculptured and elaborately serpentine, colored in horizontal bands of grey, buff, rose and maroon. ... the innumerable canyons extend into the base of Elaterite Mesa (which underlies Elaterite Butte) and into the south and southwest as far as we can see. It is like a labyrinth indeed—a labyrinth with the roof removed. (Abbey, 1968)

What likely sealed the deal for me were Abbey's parting words in the BLM register located near what is now the Hans Flat Ranger Station. Abbey wrote, "For God's sake, leave this country alone –Abbey." To which his partner added, "For Abbey's sake, leave this country alone –God" (Abbey, 1968).

I have had the privilege to visit the region of the Maze on more than one occasion. Because of the growing popularity of the area as a destination for souped-up rock crawlers, I prefer to visit the Maze in the winter when the popular Flint Trail is closed and the park is completely uninhabited by other humans. My first visit to the Maze occurred in February of 2009 when, after I drove the forty-six miles of dirt road to the Hans Flat Ranger Station, I had to search rather diligently for the only park ranger in this remote outpost to issue me a backcountry permit. It was lightly snowing as Brian wrote out my permit and told me no one had been into the Maze in over two months. As I prepared to make my way to the North Trail Canyon Trailhead, Brian had these parting words: "I hope you're self-sufficient. You're scheduled to be out on Thursday, which means I won't miss you before Friday. That means a search wouldn't begin until at least Sunday." It was actually quite encouraging to me to think that I would have the Maze completely to myself for at least a week before anyone would even notice.

North Trail Canyon drops steeply through the Orange Cliffs onto Elaterite Basin, the only access point off of Hans Flat between the Flint Trail nearly twenty miles to the south and Ekker Butte many more miles to the north. The route joins a jeep trail near Big Water Spring and begins a gradual ascent through Elaterite Basin and around the long north ridge of Elaterite Butte before it ends at the Maze Overlook. From the overlook, one sees nothing but canyon after canyon branching off into innumerable tributaries that it would take a lifetime to explore. From this point the Maze Overlook Trail, rather than resembling a trail at all, consists of little more than a controlled fall into the floor of Horse Canyon. I began my second morning again in light snow as I jumped from pour-offs, squeezed through narrow defiles, ignored the exposure of traverses around steep cliff faces, and found Moki steps carved into the sandstone to aid the descent. The silence of the desert in February is deafening as not a creature stirred and not even a breeze moved a blade of grass. I spent hours exploring like a little child, utterly amazed at something around every bend. There were natural bridges high on the rim, pothole arches not identified on a map, and the famous Harvest Scene Pictograph panel, which is one of the finest on the entire Colorado Plateau.

These were my closing words in my trip journal concerning my visit to the Maze that year: "Utterly content with a tent, my bag, tea, and my pipe on a silent evening. The last night was clear and hence cold! It is bittersweet to load up on this last day as I could spend two to three weeks exploring The Maze. Got started about 9 a.m. for the climb back up North Trail Canyon, which wasn't nearly as rough as I had anticipated. Good days of silence and solitude to refresh me for a few days. I hope to visit again soon." I had no inclination how dramatically my life would change only a month after this trip.

It's necessary at this point to pause and return to Wallace Stegner for a bit of perspective. In the introduction, Stegner was quoted as saying that particularly for Westerners, who tend to find themselves bereft of any "formed or coherent society," their first confrontations will be with landscape and hence will tend to define life based largely on such confrontations. We can extend the application, I believe, without taking too much license, if we consider not just Westerners but a whole generation of men and women who feel as if they have not been able to find a place in any coherent society. For increasing numbers of people, it is likely one's landscape that will produce perspective on life—whether good or bad. This is as true for youth in the mean streets of Detroit as it is for Native youth on a barren Navajo reservation in Arizona. I began to feel as if my own life had been formed and defined by countless days and nights spent in desert terrain. As a child, I had followed my dad for countless miles through the trackless regions of the Red Desert and Colorado Plateau. As an adult, I often chose to spend my leisure time in trips to the basins, mesas and canyons of the desert southwest. I readily accede to the idea that landscape (i.e., place) is constitutive for the soul.

The issue is how to "read" our landscape. In the months following my initial descent into the Maze, I had a particular reading of life and landscape. Places of intense wonder and wild beauty like the Maze District will inevitably impact us, and for many months, I internalized Stegner's position and began to reflect on "the devastation of this land that is becoming your soul." Growing up in the sparsely populated regions of southwest Wyoming, I was already inclined to believe that Stegner was right in saying we interpret and learn life through our landscape. It seemed to me that my life had become the desert I loved so much. At the very least, it was easy to read life through the desert view. At the time, I wrote that this view felt like "dropping into the depths of the Maze with no redemption on the horizon."

At times in the past, I have developed a sort of compulsion for visiting a particularly wild locale. In reading outdoor narratives, I would often come across a reference to a particularly wild and largely unvisited destination. I would add such a place to my mental list of trips I would need to take before I no longer had the health to do so. My initial visit to the Maze was sparked in this way by Abbey's narrative—it's as if I was driven to drop into this wild land. For many months after this initial trip, I seemed to develop another compulsion that I wrote about at the time as a strange compulsion for self-destruction. It's as if I knew my life was in disarray, and yet I was bent on dropping into a desert of the soul with nothing to offer and no release in my field of vision.

One can easily interpret the desert southwest like this, and therefore, one can also interpret one's own life if we take our cues from our landscapes. Ironically, the desert is largely defined by water—or more precisely, by the lack of usable water. Looking out across a desert scene, one is immediately drawn to how sparse and harsh the environment appears. Desert terrain is dominated by sand, gravel, and rocks. Everything is present in extremity. During summer months, temperatures soar, thinking nothing of surpassing a hundred degrees under a direct sun where the heat is intensified because of the dry atmosphere. In winter months, temperatures can plummet well below zero degrees with little escape from the bare elements. Plants and animals that do grow and live in such conditions tend to be imbued with thorns, spikes, and poisons. It is a hard place for hard creatures. Standing on a high hilltop and looking out across a desert plateau may give one the false impression that the desert is largely flat and fairly innocuous. Attempting to travel from point A to point B, however, can be an exercise in futility, and these attempts have often led to parties wandering for days. The deserts of the Colorado Plateau are cut by dry washes that become large gullies and eventually impassable slot canyons on their way to wide, inaccessible valleys rimmed in by thousand foot cliffs.

What would be the desert's salvation, water, ends up being the desert's nemesis. Falling and running water rarely absorbs into the soil of a desert environment. Instead, water moves and gathers and rushes to cut deep gashes in the earth. I have been into the very hearts of many of these defiles as they drop hundreds of feet through the sandstone, at times no wider than eighteen inches, perpetually blocking out all vision of sun and sky. Looking at the horizon line in a desert setting, travelers seem to be fixated on little other than water—a condition that the desert itself loves to play with. The heat lines that shimmer and wave above the desert floor appear as ponds or lakes, but these are merely mirages for weary, thirsty travelers. When late summer storm clouds do build in the west, they are merely a tease that offers little hope and less relief. Summer storms often evaporate in midair before they can nourish the soil. When rain does fall in the desert, it is far more likely to create devastation rather than provide relief. Flash floods cut into the earth, uprooting entire trees and rolling boulders the size of cars down thick rivers of mud.

Growing up, I had always learned to refer to the late summer season as "monsoon season." Every afternoon around 2:00 p.m., like clockwork, clouds would build, and a brief thunderstorm would explode on the scene and quickly move out. In *The Secret Knowledge of Water*, Craig Childs says,

> What we have in the southwest is more a season
> of chubascos than monsoons. If a monsoon is a
> big front of weather [monsoons are broad and
> slow rain-storms, liquefying the ground into
> mud, sweeping over entire continents like an arm
> brushing crumbs from a table] then chubascos

are needles poking through the weather map. A chubasco is a kind of storm that eats holes into the sky and the earth. It is a convective thunderstorm, the one item of weather that brings the quickest rainfall, the heaviest winds, and erodes the most land.(Childs, 2000)

These features made it easy for me to look out across a desert and see no redemption in sight. The harsh and devastated landscape was an appropriate characterization of my life for many months. Prior to my descent into the Maze in February of 2009, I had been struggling with a loss of my own identity. I had recently left vocational ministry, where I had spent years in schooling, training, and practice living in the intellectual realm of theology and church life. I found myself working in the oil field on a drilling rig, wondering if the life of the mind had been pursued to my benefit or not. In March of 2009, because of one of the many familiar "busts" in the ever-present boom/bust cycle of the oil field, I found myself laid off from work, and so my ability to employ my work ethic for the sake of my family was stripped from me as well. It wasn't long before I sensed an almost entire loss of myself as I descended into utter chaos. I felt bent on pursuing a drop into a harsh, unforgiving land. The desert made sense to me with its apparent lack of redemption on the horizon.

Our landscapes, whatever those happen to be, can be read in this way. Nature has a way of asserting her independence in ways that often seem rather devastating to our own comfort and sense of order. Stegner accedes to such a dearth of the desert environment, but he also reads the apparent lack of human-oriented comforts in a very different way. "The Utah deserts and plateaus and canyons are not a country of big returns, but a country of spiritual healing, incomparable for contemplation, meditation, solitude, quiet and peace of mind and body. We were born of wilderness and we respond to it more increasingly for relief from the termite life we have created" (Stegner, 1998). I failed to understand at the time that I saw no redemption and couldn't get my feeble life together and find perspective because I was only living a sort of half-life.

I returned to the Maze again in February 2011. This winter was again an experience of wild solitude as I scared the solitary ranger nearly to death because she hadn't seen a backpacker for months and still wasn't expecting any for months to follow. I followed my previous route down North Trail Canyon, across Elaterite Basin, and down from the Maze Overlook on foot. This winter, however, I ascended a trail out of Horse Canyon to the rim of Jasper Canyon—one of the many canyons that make up the Maze District—and found myself interpreting life in light of the desert in a very different way. Jasper Canyon lies deep in the heart of the Maze. It flows for miles from south to north, rimmed by inaccessibly high cliffs as it makes its way to a high pour-off into the Green River. Jasper Canyon has never been commercially grazed because of its inaccessibility, and so it remains a prime example of a pristine environment virtually untouched by human interference. The National Park Service considers this canyon to be an environmental benchmark and consequently has closed all access to the canyon for backpackers. I followed the high west rim of the canyon for miles to the north and found myself in humble awe of this untouched land. Canyons such as these are a pleasure to view from high above on the canyon rim because of the breadth of view a high vantage point allows. I was able to view groves of cottonwoods in winter sleep, side canyons branching off for miles in every direction, deep and contrasting colors creating stratified bands on the cliff walls, even a small game trail snaking its way through the canyon floor. My pleasure and perspective of this desert topography was not due to trip conditions that were friendlier than the ones I experienced two years previous. I spent my nights sleeping in the open air under clear skies. The temperature plummeted to ten degrees. What had changed was a healing integration that had begun to occur in my life a few months before.

Throughout history, many authors have often interpreted the desert as a harsh and unforgiving place, and consequently, they tend to equate this reality with "desert experiences" in which life seems to dry up and wither away. It is indeed a hard environment—again, the irony being how it is defined by something too often absent. But it is precisely the hard nature of the desert that creates its stark and hypnotizing beauty. When the rushing, flooding waters do come, they cut twisting slots through layers of sandstone and reveal contrasting colors that play with the scant light from a mere slit of sky. Rainfall running down sheer cliff faces mixes with minerals in the rock and creates dark stripes of falling "desert varnish," which gives miles of sheer cliff walls color and texture. Over centuries, the ever-present wind and the hard rains have created massive detached towers, arches, and rock bridges over trickling springs. Infrequent springs emanating from deep in the earth provide an oasis for towering cottonwoods that seem to glow with a vibrant green precisely because of the contrast with the reds, tans, and grays of the landscape. Seeps issuing from high on the canyon walls produce alcoves and sprawling, hanging gardens. The smallest orange, purple, or yellow from tiny flowers command greater attention because of how surprising they appear in such conditions. Like Muggeridge would affirm, the complexity, weight, and hardship is precisely what contains the desert's beauty.

John Van Dyke was one of the first to write in appreciation of the American desert. *The Desert* was published in 1901, and it takes the very harsh and sparse nature of the desert as the key to its own special beauty. It is the absence of shining rivers and flashing lakes, the shadows of foliage, and the sound of running waters that makes the desert what it is, and while poets may not be drawn to such realities, the desert can be read as beautiful and right in its own way. It is a peculiar beauty not to be romanticized or trivialized. "It is a great land of splintered peaks, torn valleys, and hot skies. And at every step there is the suggestion of the fierce, the defiant, the defensive. Everything within its borders seems fighting to maintain itself against destroying forces." Van Dyke affirms that the fierce quality of the desert is precisely what makes it so attractive.

> What is it that draws us to the boundless and fathomless? Why should the lovely things of earth—the grasses, the trees, the lakes, the little hills—appear trivial and insignificant when we come face to face with the sea or the desert or the vastness of the midnight sky? Is it that the one is the tale of things known and the other merely a hint, a suggestion of the unknown? Or have immensity, space, magnitude a peculiar beauty of their own? Is it not true that bulk and breadth are primary and essential qualities of the sublime in landscape? And is it not the sublime

that we feel in immensity and mystery? If so, perhaps we have a partial explanation for our love for sky and sea and desert waste. They are the great elements. We do not see, we hardly know, if their boundaries are limited; we only feel their immensity, their mystery, and their beauty. (Van Dyke, 1901)

The landscape I had visited two years apart was the same; the difference was that I was learning to read life in light of that landscape in a very different way. I had recently begun to spend time with Bob, my friend and counselor, and he was able to quickly pinpoint my issue. I was only living from a sort of half-life. There was very little, if any integration between the various elements of my being. Bob began by talking about Jesus' teaching as presented by his biographer Mark when he said the most important thing in life is to "love the Lord your God with all your heart and with all your soul and with all your mind and with all your strength" (Mark 12:30). Regardless of your own sense or absence of religious life, any of us can recognize the genius of Jesus' words as he encourages us to respond to the gift of life by responding in love with our whole being. I don't believe that Jesus was intending to provide a scientific perspective on a human being's physiology; however, his insight into the various ways we come to life is profound. In one sentence, he addresses our emotions, our souls or spiritual lives, our intellect, and our physicality. To be able to balance and integrate those ways of showing up in the world is the great challenge of life.

It was in this light that I was introduced to the work of Robert Moore and Douglas Gillette through their book *King,*

Warrior, Magician, Lover: Rediscovering the Archetypes of the Mature Masculine. Moore and Gillette's archetypes correspond to the far more ancient wisdom of Jesus. The king is the part of us that directs and blesses the other elements. It is our soul. The warrior is our physical portion, responsible for action and battle. The magician corresponds to our mind and our intellectual endeavors. The lover is characterized by our emotional life. The authors identify many of our contemporary crises with the failure to understand the presence of these four archetypes and the corresponding lack of maturity in dealing with and expressing our souls, our often violent physicality, our intellectual efforts, and our emotional need for love. Balance and healthy integration are crucial. "The four major forms of the mature masculine energies we have identified are the King, the Warrior, the Magician and the Lover. They all overlap and, ideally, enrich one another. A good King is always also a Warrior, a Magician, and a lover. And the same holds for the other three" (Moore and Gillette, 1990).

I have already shared at length the lifelong sense of worthlessness and the fear I harbored that I never really belonged in the world of mature masculine men, a level of acceptance that I assumed most around me had already attained. As my means of dealing with this kind of life, I engaged fully in the life of the mind at the expense of my soul and particularly my emotions. At some point early in my life, I endeavored to accept what I perceived were accurate judgments on my value, and the wounded sage was born as a protective element. I spent over three decades developing the life of the mind in an effort to not only hide myself *from* myself but also gain some credibility through "expertise." There was no sovereign (i.e., soul) to direct traffic for my development and bring a physical life into balance with an emotional and intellectual one; the emotional life for me harbored too many risks to really delve into. I studied and attended school and sought a profession where I might be perceived as having answers and being something important. All the while, the wounded sage was making judgments on my reality from a mere half-life, judgments that where I was or what I was doing was never good enough and couldn't possibly be what life was supposed to be about.

Throughout the discussion thus far, it should be apparent that many of the crucial expressions of a healthy understanding of life in the cultural context we inhabit go directly against the grain of how many of us are making our ways through this world. Complexity, weight, and fear are things we typically attempt to remove from or reduce in our lives in order to make more comfortable ways. We have seen how detrimental ignoring the presence of these realities can be for existence. Grasping and thriving in a healthy psyche is no less counterintuitive. Each archetype of the "mature masculine" has its own "gateway emotion" that allows access to the deeper and richer health of the whole person. Fear is the gateway into the sage or magician archetype. Grief leads us into the fullness of the lover, and anger allows us to touch the warrior. Ironically, these are some of the emotional elements that our own context has so successfully eliminated from our experience.

Whereas many ancient cultures would have been fed a regular diet of fear, grief, and anger, we have little or no context for how critical these emotions are. I believe that to a large degree our societal malaise is simply a product of our cultural conditioning. As we progress through life, it is likely that we have failed to realize that these natural experiences are necessary in order for humans to find the healthy path to integration. We are not allowed to explore or experience fear, anger, and grief in healthy ways because our own culture primarily fixates only on the negative sides of these emotions. From a relatively young age, we are taught to repress our anger, move on from our grief, and get over our fear. The problem then becomes not the absence of any one element but our ability to recognize it as such and to internalize the benefit of such an emotion.

The reality is that each of us will experience fear, grief, and anger at some point. As we are taught to repress or ignore these emotions, however, they bury themselves deep in our psyches and tend to express themselves primarily in unhealthy ways. An associated problem can then manifest itself in the overabundance of only one emotion, which asserts itself at the expense of any sort of balance. Herein we return to our primary idea of life as a sojourn and how we pack for the journey. My own pack had long been overflowing with an unrecognized fear, the gateway emotion to a life of the mind, which left little room to experience or understand appropriate grief (and hence emotions) or anger. As we look over the landscape of postmodern America, we can easily recognize many individuals carrying the same kinds of loads, albeit loads full of different things. Many of us know overly feminine males who seem to exist on a steady diet of little more than emotion. This behavior is likely the product of carrying some kind of unrecognized grief throughout life with no healthy context in which to process such emotion. In a book on male spirituality, Richard Rohr is careful to distinguish such unhealthy inwardness and femininity (which he rightly calls a "false feminine") from a healthy emotional and spiritual life balanced by action and physicality.

For the past several years, I have worked in one of the most dangerous industries in America. I have spent countless hours in sweltering heat and subzero temperatures, working on a drilling rig, pushing heavy iron around through grease and mud in western Colorado. This kind of industry has long been the setting of choice for hard men who more often than not come from hard lives. The industry is one dominated by the physical, and it often attracts men for whom there is little other expression for life than its sheer physicality. It is not surprising to come across a large number of angry people (because the emotion of anger serves as a gateway to the warrior mentality) who are often the way they are as the result of traveling through life with a pack full of unprocessed rage, likely stemming from some event in their youth they could neither control nor understand. When the crew that I have been a part of for the past couple of years shares hugs and exclamations of appreciation all around at the end of our fourteen-day hitch, many others in our midst are surprised at even a small expression of emotion. Those who have long dwelt in an environment dominated by only the physical have little capacity to understand anything else.

It was a far different environment, however, for the two decades preceding my work in the gas fields of Colorado. The American church seems to be centered on and dominated by the life of the mind. I spent six years in an educational system teaching me how to conjugate Greek verbs and formulate systematic doctrines of theology. It causes me to reflect now on how much of the church may be dominated by fear—a fear of not making the grade, not being good enough, or not being smart enough to have the answers for a confused and disordered world. I remember my Greek professor from my undergrad days warning his students to carefully check their own motivations in entering a "helping" profession such as full-time vocational ministry. He told us that if we were entering the ministry to compensate for some kind of personal deficiency, we were not likely to make it. I wonder how many others delved into this life of the mind as the only access point they had to life emerging primarily out of fear.

The above scenes from life are simply meant as illustrations of how we can travel through life with a bag packed with an overabundance of one emotion to the detriment of any other, giving rise to the absence of balance. Exceptions certainly exist in any venue of life, but they remain just that, exceptions. Our parents, teachers, and mentors have done us a grave disservice if they have convinced us of only the negative consequences of grief, anger, and fear without helping us understand their crucial role in opening us to the ability to respond to life out of all the areas Jesus encourages us to, specifically our minds, our bodies, our hearts, and our spirits.

I have really only begun to piece together a long series of events that has started to work toward my own sense of integration. I share this journey not as a template for others to attempt to plug the elements of their own lives into but simply as an attempt to help other individuals recognize that the movement toward healthy balance often contains many episodes that we need to become attune to. It is crucial that we begin to recognize some of the scenes from our lives that may be nudging us toward health. For me, such inclinations had been present for years, but I had no system or language for recognizing what was emerging in my life. Things only came together when I was able to personally experience the four major forms of the "mature masculine" present in my own life. What I found was that much of my need for integration through a healthy experience of emotions centered on the latent love for my dad.

It wasn't long after my dad's death that I was traveling across the open, rolling hills of western Iowa on my way to a meeting when my Eagles's *Greatest Hits* CD came across their song "Desperado." This was a favorite song of my dad's, and we had even played it at his funeral a few months earlier. In some ways, it seems that the song was written specifically for him, and I found myself playing it over and over again as it offered me a bit of perspective into his life. As I drove alone through the early morning hours, an overwhelming sense of grief descended on my vehicle. It wasn't long before I was weeping uncontrollably, the tears clouding my vision of the road ahead. This was perhaps the first time since my dad had died that I had openly grieved about the loss. My tears lasted a full half hour before they abruptly ceased. Because I didn't have much experience with grief and the strength of my own emotions at this point, I felt a strange guilt after I was so expressive. I forced myself to regain my composure, and the brief introduction to my latent grief and the opening of my emotions were tucked safely back into the folds of a busy life.

Perhaps a year later, I was driving through the sagebrush and scrub oak country of western Colorado on my way to a committee meeting while I was listening to the Pink Floyd album *Wish You Were Here*. (I have since come to realize that music is often an important doorway into my own buried emotional life). The album was released in 1975, and it was nearly an instant number-one record on British Billboard Charts (and then in the United States a few weeks later). David Gilmore sings on the title track, "How I wish, how I wish you were here. We're just two lost souls swimming in a fish bowl, year after year. Running over the same old ground, and have we found the same old fears? Wish you were here." I again thought of my dad and my own wish that he was still around to discuss things like life and its resident fears. I was already beginning to feel a certain restlessness about life, which I know plagued him to a certain extent as well, and I was wondering if I would eventually travel the same ground that he had, as if life were that small fishbowl I would continue to circle with no other view. It was my initial realization that we might very well have shared some of the same fears about our own place (or nonplace) in the world.

Like many others my own age, I desperately needed these emotions to come together in a way that might bring about integration in my life, which up to this point had been rather disconnected and random. My emotional life consisted of isolated incidents and expressions of brief insight into what I might need, but insight which rarely made the transition into the whole of life and even less often came to any fruition of clarity. The crucial turning point for me came one afternoon in Bob's office when I openly acknowledged the fear that had plagued me throughout my life. The important thing to note is that I didn't simply say, "This is the fear that drives my life," but I allowed it to actually sink deeply into my being, where I could see it for what it was and what it had done to me over the past three decades.

Bob was patient enough to shepherd me through the process of allowing this fear to set heavily on my heart when I began to shed copious tears. Because I wasn't adept at emotional outbreaks, it made me angry to think that I was losing my otherwise stoical presence. Grief poured forth at the loss of so many years of healthy being as well as rage at being somehow cheated out of a life that had digressed to little more than pain at this point. I was blubbering and swearing and raging. What I was actually doing was finding a place in my life's pack for emotions and anger and fear. In this context, my soul finally surfaced in my life in the very real feeling of a solid core being placed in the center of my being. There was finally a seed of integration. The gateway emotions to the king, the lover, the warrior, and the sage had finally given me access to a fullness one element never could.

This was a critical turning point for my life. The acknowledgment of fear, the understanding healthy anger, and the expression of grief all led to the sense that for the first time, I had access to my soul. Finding our spiritual selves, our souls, is crucial because this discovery can then be associated with the king in the image of Moore and Gillette. As the authors state in their study on the male psyche,

> The King archetype in its fullness possesses the qualities of order, of reasonable and rational patterning, of integration and integrity in the masculine psyche. It stabilizes chaotic emotion and out-of-control behaviors. It gives stability and centeredness. It brings calm. And in its 'fertilizing' and centeredness, it mediates vitality, life-force and joy. It brings maintenance and balance. It defends our own sense of inner order, our own integrity of being and purpose, our own central calmness about who we are. (Moore and Gillette, 1990)

This is what we have always been searching for through all of our reaching efforts for success and reputation. It is important for us to recognize that the entry points to the ordering elements in our lives are accessed through our fear, our grief, and our anger. Despite what our culture conditions us to believe, grief, anger, and fear do not have to be primarily negative experiences if they can be ordered and centered through the presence of the king.

The central metaphor of wild places, perhaps especially that of the desert environment, again becomes vital at just this point. In his presentation on early desert monasticism, Belden Lane points out that desert fathers and mothers retreated to wild places precisely because these were the contexts where an accurate understanding and integration of one's life was most likely to occur. "Ultimately, they chose to live in a desert habitat because they knew how well it teaches, without even trying, the importance of being emptied, the spiritual lessons of kenosis" (Lane, 1998). Of particular importance in Lane's discussion is how the desert is specifically adept at emptying the self of inaccuracies and delusions about life in the world. The desert has a unique ability to fill even while it empties— the interesting juxtaposition of perspective we have already encountered in John Van Dyke and Wallace Stegner.

What desert monastics realized was their need to be emptied and set free from an undue preoccupation with themselves and how they might appear to other people in reputation and accomplishment. The sparse environment of the desert allowed them to set aside a debilitating selfward orientation through its own harsh and seemingly "threatening indifference," and yet this was precisely the means of coming to a free and integrated life. Lane believes that it was precisely the harsh and severe aspects of the desert which were sought by desert monastics as the necessary elements to lead one to spiritual and emotional health.

> They knew that only the most unrelenting discipline, echoing the desert's harshness, could deal with the subtle deceptions of the ego. The grand indifference of limestone crags and wormwood served as an effective antidote to all delusions of self-importance. The ancient desert had persisted for eons prior to their coming and would continue long after their death. ... The desert monks were hardly naïve despisers of culture. What they fled with greatest fear was not the external world, but the world they carried inside themselves: an ego-centeredness needing constant approval, driven by compulsive behavior, frantic in its effort to attend to a self-image that always required mending. (Lane, 1998)

Upon reflection, I look back and realize that my repeated trips to regions like the Maze serve my own life in these instructive ways.

I can't believe that my situation is really all that unique. Because so few of us have appropriately been initiated into the mature masculine archetypes, many reach the middle point of life and feel utterly stuck. No one seems to be directing traffic, and the emotional parts of our lives seem too seldom engaged in the flow of our lives. Men most often compensate for the grief of the lover through the anger of the warrior or the fear of the sage. This is why careers are so crucial to us. They give us a comfortable and safe environment to engage either our bodies or our minds. We really don't know how to live any other way. We need integration if we hope to stop this aimless drift through life.

If we are lucky enough to pay attention to life, we will recognize the dissolution when it sets in, which it inevitably will for so many of us raised without fathers in the Age of Entitlement—usually somewhere around forty years old, but for a fortunate few, maybe even closer to thirty. It begins as a nagging feeling that things somehow aren't right, that all is not as it should be. There is usually some mild depression we can't seem to shake ourselves free from, not even after we have bought new things, taken trips, moved to other homes, or changed our careers. However we try to address the malaise, it only helps for a brief time, and we wonder if the merry-go-round simply keeps turning us in circles up to our dying day.

This is the life's call for integration. We risk significant damage to the self if we ignore the cultivation of a life balanced physically, mentally, emotionally and spiritually. Because the body depends on the mind and both rely so heavily on the emotional life for motivation and protection, things will eventually start crying to be recognized. Somewhere in our closed-off half-lives, we can recognize a sort of strange compulsion that seems to drive many of us to strange places we've never been and likely don't know what to do with. I started writing about this sense of compulsion early on in my own dissolution, and at the time, I wasn't even sure why. I remember feeling and writing as if I was compelled to run at breakneck speed into my own self-destruction, and in the process, I was burning everything down around me. I recognized a sort of constraint pushing me forward, even if it all seemed so destructive, but I had met the dissolution of life and something had to change. I remember sitting in an Irish pub in Colorado Springs one afternoon when a TV commercial struck me, advertising for something I cannot even remotely recall. The byline said, "Let's light ourselves on fire and plummet off a high-rise." No longer could my mind prop me up, and no longer was my work ethic sufficient to convince me that everything was okay. This strange sense of what I call "compulsion" was my life crying to be whole.

At the same time that I was trying to sort out this sense of being driven forward, I look back and see that I was also writing about wanting to be whole. It just took me too many months to connect the dots. I remembered the stories of Jesus touching lepers and washing the sand from his disciples' feet—acts steeped in the physical soil of life where it was lived. I wondered if too much of our religion caused us to attempt to live above the fray—too otherworldly and "spiritual" to be bothered by everyday life. I reflected on Thoreau, who said he went to the woods because he "wanted to live deliberately." I had long been a fan of the writings of Ed Abbey and the literature of Russia because they all seemed to be rooted in a real experience of the soil of life. The coffee I enjoyed and the kind of beer I drank tended to be strong and bitter—the kind that leaves an experience and memory on the back of the palate. I recognize now that my headlong flight into something different from what I had built was a broken and misguided attempt to find a life lived from the emotional, physical, intellectual, and spiritual places of the self.

If we don't recognize that the disintegration in these moments is actually life's cry for integration and wholeness, then we are likely to spend months, if not years, of utter frustration trying to make sense of where we are. Simply changing the scenery isn't likely to help. For months, I thought I was moving into a more organic form of life, and I convinced myself that my emotional life was beginning to blossom. As I look back over numerous journal entries, however, it seemed as if I was viewing my life as an outsider, watching circumstances unfold on the movie screen of a theater.

> Now it all seems so unreal, as if my life were a movie I am watching happen around me, seated in the theater seats, watching all of these strange circumstances happen on the stage or screen but mostly detached from what is actually happening to me and others in my circle. The dialogue from too many people seems as if it were spoken to someone else. And it even seems as if the film will run its course to a conclusion while I sit back in the seats and watch it happen.

These certainly are not the words of a man engaged and present in his situation. I doubt that this is an entirely unique circumstance as we watch so many men and women reach their crises and respond with new jobs, addictions, or relationships, all the while taking their broken and unassimilated lives with them.

This is the place where the things we've learned thus far about life actually begin to make a difference. To receive life as a complex, weighty thing imbued with fear is to move toward being a whole person. I shared in the discussion about weight how I experienced the deposit of something in my very being, and I believe this was the realization of my soul. This was largely the result of acknowledging the presence of fear and how that had expressed itself in my life. Grief was allowed to come to expression, and I understood the value of the warrior being freed and equipped to fight so that a path for a whole life might be opened. The sovereign (i.e., the soul) was again present to direct traffic and bring life into balance.

This is an important concept to grasp because of how it impinges on our spiritual lives. Apart from integration, one's spiritual life will tend to be expressed in one of two poles. It can look like the quest for a controlling order in which religion and spirituality exist only as intellectual exercises wherein we are bent on systematizing mystery and forming some kind of easy-to-follow guidebook that looks more like us than that which nothing greater can be conceived. For many, on the other hand, the life of the soul is little more than emotional chaos, which tends to swing wildly in intense highs and lows. Balance (complexity) is the key in this all-important realm. We must learn to respond to God with our minds, bodies, and hearts all directed by the solid core of the soul. Richard Rohr says, "A masculine spirituality would emphasize action over theory, service to the human community over religious discussions, speaking the truth over social graces and doing justice over looking nice. Without a complimentary masculine, spirituality becomes overly feminine (which is really a false feminine) and is characterized by too much inwardness, preoccupation with relationships, a morass of unclarified feeling and endless self-protection" (Rohr, 1996).

If we can pay attention long enough, we will find that it is in the liminal spaces of life that we are most apt to come face-to-face with the complex, heavy, and fearful reality of a full life. Life tends to be littered with these "edge" experiences, which

I believe represent the presence of God attempting to get our attention. One of our problems is how adept we have become at softening these edges or completely insulating ourselves from such experiences through our engineered and comfortable lives. In *Adam's Return*, a book about male spirituality, Richard Rohr writes,

> The Latin word *limen* means "threshold." Liminality is an inner state and sometimes outer situation where people can begin to think and act in genuinely new ways. It is when we are betwixt and between, have left one room but not yet entered the next room ... It is that graced time when we are not certain or in control, when something genuinely new can happen. We are empty, receptive, an erased tablet waiting for new words. Nothing fresh or creative will normally happen when we are inside our self-constructed comfort zones, only more of the same ... It seems we need some anti-structure to give direction, depth, and purpose to our regular structure. (Rohr, 2004)

Wild, uninhabited places are contexts for finding such liminal space. Times spent in the wilderness can provide us with these edge experiences, and if we are teachable, they can help us integrate before it's too late. If you spend much time reading adventure narratives or talking to people who spend much time outdoors, a common theme seems to be how life-affirming it often is to be on the edge of one's resources. Taking your food, water, mental and physical capacities to the very brink has a way of revealing you to yourself, and it also has the capacity to produce clarity of thought so you can potentially "think and act in genuinely new ways." To sojourn into a mountain or desert wilderness is to cultivate a liminal space in life outside of normal comfort zones. Lately, I have found myself seeking out harder trips—trail less canyons, longer paths, mountains in the winter, or deserts in the summer. Such experiences have less to do with some kind of thrill in the adventure and more to do with the deep need to find liminal space where greater integration of my spiritual, physical, emotional, and intellectual life can occur.

The words of Michael Wolcott in a recent article for *Mountain Gazette* resonate sharply with me in this regard. Although a lengthy quote, I believe its eloquence stands out sharper than my own could.

> Something gnaws in my belly. It never goes away. I don't need to see a doctor. The Cat scans and barium dye, the blood and tissue samples— none of it is necessary. All along I've known what this thing inside me is. I don't need a medical opinion. For years I've been walking in the dry places, following unpromising washes, looking under rocks. I sleep in the mouths of played-out copper mines and stare at sunrise over the rim of a charred steel coffee cup, sure of my self-diagnosis: terminal hunger. Walking in the desert is my preferred treatment for this malady, a basic ingratitude for the ease and abundance of my life. (Wolcott, 2012)

In this sense, the small tracts of wild places still available to us can serve as the "training grounds" for edge experiences and integrated lives. We need such experiences to prepare us for those times in life when everything seems to be dissolving and we are tempted to abandon whatever darkness we many find ourselves in. In 1911, an ill-advised expedition was launched in Antarctica with the intention to study the natural patterns of penguins. The study occurred during the winter months in almost complete darkness. Disaster after disaster met the party, and the expedition had to complete a sixty-seven-mile walk in the night of an Antarctic winter. Tom Griffiths says, "The men hauled their sledges for 19 days and Cherry-Gerard could not find the words to describe the horror of that night-time epic: 'They talk of the heroism of the dying—they little know—it would be so easy to die, a dose of morphine, a friendly crevasse, and blissful sleep. The trouble is to go on'" (Griffiths, 2007). If we've never learned that we can go on and survive episodes like this, what is to keep us from checking out of life through abandonment of the struggle or the numbing effects of some kind of substance?

I wish I could say that I have always had this conscious sense of why I felt so compelled to travel to uninhabited places during the times I did make such trips. It took me years, however, to realize that trips to the wilderness were critical for me because these were often the only places I actually felt whole during those years when I was living only a sort of half-life. A trip begins by engaging my intellect as I pour over maps and often check trail reports or accounts of previous visits (if there are any). I plan menus and think through the necessary gear and pack carefully to keep the weight of my pack as light as possible while I still have what I might need. There is a definite physicality involved as I have learned to appreciate the very act of walking, climbing, setting up, and dismantling camp—

even in those times when I have no definite objective or a planned destination cannot be reached. The physical fatigue is a rewarding feeling in and of itself. When I didn't know how to engage my emotions in the rest of life, they would often blossom in primitive settings, producing something akin to the giddiness of a child as I wondered over high red walls, sweeping summit views, or even the simple pleasures of wild raspberries or a bright Indian paintbrush. The presence of an awakened physical, intellectual, and emotional life more often than not produced a soul that was alive, a spirituality I couldn't produce elsewhere because I was less than whole and far more guarded when I was back in a less-than-natural setting.

My wife, Colleen, has attested to this on more than one occasion. Colleen is an amazing woman and a great mother, but she is not necessarily inclined to spend weeks on end sleeping on the ground and cooking over a fire. Still, she looks forward to our family outings because she has long known these do something significant for me. She has told me how much more patient and relaxed I am in the hills, recognizing even before I did that I was a better person to be around when I was living out of an integrated wholeness. It is the "solace of fierce landscapes" I have always sought when I didn't know what else to do with life. After I endured a particularly stressful season at the district office in Omaha and after I gave my notice (the first time), I was sent alone to the Indian Peaks Wilderness for some perspective. Following the dissolution of the avalanche, the family loaded up for a week in the southern Utah desert. When life makes no sense, I know I can always go to the wilderness, engage my whole being, and begin to feel a sense of integration again.

What I am coming to understand is that these "edges" need to be moved into the central places of the rest of life. If wilderness has served as a metaphor for life, then the lessons learned there need to be applied and laid over the top of a whole life. For years, I have kept a trip journal in which I record my adventures and responses, even chronicling weather and trail conditions so that I can continue to picture the experience and learn what it is saying to me. Those are important contexts for us to learn how to deal with weight and fear and how to express emotions and even let them spill out of us. I am learning to recognize the familiar presence of fear when I am confronted by a mistake and when I immediately revert to the defensiveness produced by the sense of being revealed as worthless because I have somehow come up short. The integration born of wilderness helps me say, "I've felt this before! And I think I can keep climbing through it to see what's on the other side."

I am seeing now that fatigue is often simply an automatic response I experience when my unexercised emotional life is required to be present, perhaps on an evening when things quiet down and my wife needs my emotional engagement more than physical contact. From many miles logged in the backcountry, I know the best way to deal with fatigue is to walk on, not seek to lie down and disengage. Our fatigue is often feigned as we find ourselves too tired to emotionally engage, yet we can watch television or read a book for hours late into the night. What does a man do when he finds himself alone and many miles from the Elkhart Park, Woodenshoe, or Hans Flat trailhead? There is little else to do other than walk. And at the end of a hard day, water has to be filtered, a tent set up, dinner cooked. And we do these things because survival and health depend on them. This is part of learning to layer the life of wilderness over the rest of life. We recognize things like our feigned fatigue. We walk into the weariness, and therefore, we head toward emotional connection and integration. Visits to wild places are not simply about another form of "unplugging" or entertainment in an already oversaturated and overstimulated life. They are about edge experiences where the king, warrior, sage, and lover can be present and recognized so that a full, integrated life can be shared with those in our context.

It is crucial at this point in history to reengage with the things that will bring us healthy integration back into life. Societal issues stem largely from the deeper personal crises faced by modern men and women. We have simply lost the sense of where balance might be found for the various chaotic and unattached aspects of our beings. Too often the older we get, the less sense we seem to be able to make of life. In his work on place and journey in Celtic spirituality, Philip Sheldrake points out the balance and harmony present in a great many themes of Celtic life without unduly romanticizing their culture. Part of their strength was found in a sense that life itself was liminal space. It constituted an entire boundary or edge experience where the membrane between the spiritual and the physical was actually quite thin. Place was important because physical contexts could actually connect the material world with the intangible, the seen with the unseen. "The understanding of nature in Celtic spirituality arises from a sense of living within a 'cosmos of the edge.' Human places, natural features and landscapes are at the same time the concrete world of our daily experience in which we consciously live and yet something more. They also constitute a world of wonder, power, spirits, and God" (Sheldrake, 1995).

This is why wilderness is so critical for us and why it often remains as one of the last places for us to discover what integration, harmony, and balance might actually look like for the daily lives we lead. Sheldrake reminds us that "our understanding of the spatio-temporal or 'place' and 'placedness' is crucial to the ways we formulate and live our spiritualties." The enlivened life of the soul will inevitably be tied to the places we find ourselves in or can bring ourselves to visit. More than ever, we need to cultivate some liminal space where the membranes are thin if we hope to integrate who we really are within ourselves. "[A]n engagement with 'place' may enable a spiritual inner journey. The journey of the wandering ascetics was actually a search for the ultimate place, a place of harmony and the unity of all things in the absolute—what Celtic ascetics called 'the place of resurrection'" (Sheldrake, 1995). It is likely time for many of us to undertake a journey to the edge.

> *Desert and mountain places are often associated with the "limit-experiences" of people on the edge, people who have run out of language in speaking of God, people whose recourse to fierce landscapes has fed some deep need within them for the abandonment of control and the acceptance of God's love in absolute, unmitigated grace.*
> —BELDON LANE, THE SOLACE OF FIERCE LANDSCAPES

CONCLUSION

Live your lives here as one continuously
walking from his home.
—1 PETER 2:11

Y EARS AGO, I was part of a team that organized and led six-day backpacking adventures for high school and college students. Many of the students joining us had never been involved in trips that covered so many miles on foot deep into a primitive setting. To carry one's home, bed, and a week's worth of food was more often than not a significant life-changing event for many participants. Before each endeavor, we took great pains to clue these students in to the experience they were about to enjoy, casting wilderness trips like these as microcosms of life. Individuals were told that they were likely to experience the total spectrum of emotional and physical change in the span of a few days. There would be elation, enthusiasm, and energy to be followed sometimes quickly by fatigue, frustration and even disillusionment at the thought of being so deep in the wilderness. We knew that everyone at some point would feel utterly worn out and on the edge of both physical and emotional reserves. By way of confession, it was actually this state that we purposefully hoped to introduce to youth after the first two grueling days, knowing that this was precisely the state where they would be most teachable. Reflecting on those trips, students inevitably discovered beauty in pain and realized the best scenery was found far from roads in places one must search to reach. There was always joy on the other side.

Wilderness travel is truly a microcosm of life. This is why sojourning can help us deal with the ever-present and seemingly all-consuming issue of expectations. Too many of us have no idea how to respond to a life near forty, that stubbornly refuses to meet the expectations we placed on it when we were twenty. What happens when we wake up and find ourselves not as successful (or maybe worse, more successful), fulfilled, or simply as well adjusted as we had planned to be in our middle years? We can ignore the reality, lash out in dangerous ways, and seek to numb ourselves to the epiphany, or hopefully, we can spend the next few years learning to respond to the complexity that is life and allow it to add weight to the rest of our years so that we might emerge in the late fall of life as people of substance.

When I was a few years younger, I headed out for a solo attempt on Gannett Peak's rarely climbed west side via the Minor Glacier. My approach entailed a backpack up the narrow defile of Wells Creek out of Three Forks Park on the Green River. The guidebook has the following to say about the Wells Creek approach:

A disproportionate amount of the criticism that was accorded the 1980 guidebook was inspired by its depiction of Wells Creek. A reviewer who admitted to being one of many mountaineering greats turned back by the rugged chasm, condemned the entire book because of this passage:

> The route up Wells Creek has suffered a bad reputation, with tales of impassable cliffs and direct aid; certainly the view from below offers no encouragement. The cleft is probably impassable early in the summer when the creek is high. Leave the Highline Trail near the upper end of Three Forks Park and ford the Green and ascend the right side of Wells Creek. Enter the cleft and climb near the waterfalls, crossing the creek when necessary. Inexperienced climbers may need a rope on a few of the large boulders.

While these are the facts, you may, while you are struggling up the cleft, require grimmer prose: expect 15-foot boulders and 5.5 moves. Unless you seek the adventure of one of the Range's severest backpacks, consider Tourist Creek which is less malignant than Wells Creek yet rugged enough to inspire curses at this guide. (Kelsey, 1994)

I made my way up the Green River and onto Wells Creek where I found the going rugged, though far from impassable, until I ascended to the narrowest portion of the creek which was in full force, blowing glacial melt over a twenty-foot waterfall. I was virtually at the top of the canyon where Wells Creek flows out of Scott Lake, and I refused to believe that after the morning's efforts and the peak looming merely a day or two beyond, I could actually be turned away. I was loaded with a four-day pack when I attempted to climb the vertical face on the right side of the waterfall. About halfway up, I was feeling increasingly nervous when I noticed a piton someone had driven into the wall to attach climbing protection to. The realization that I was in a bad spot barely preceded the horror as the vertical slabs I was hanging from came detached from the cliff. I fell nearly fifteen feet, barely catching a wide spot on the bank before I would have been plunged into Wells Creek and likely later found floating in the Green River flowing far below. I was bloody and bruised and sat on the bank of the roaring torrent of the creek and simply wept. My expectations had not been met. Things were not going according to my plan, and instead of dealing appropriately with the situation, I had tried to force my way through to my goal. I was angry, alone, miles from the trailhead, and scared to death from the fall. If we don't learn to deal rightly with frustrated expectations, we will inevitably end up bruised and broken … or worse.

More recently I was making my way up a rugged canyon in Utah's Cedar Mesa when I was stopped by a beautiful dry fall that had created a pothole arch where floodwaters would plunge through during thunderstorms. I was sure that there was a way through the canyon, but I had missed a critical high-ledge system only accessible from far back down the canyon. In contrast to my earlier Gannett experience, however, I decided against an effort to force my way to the upper reaches of the canyon. Instead, I found a small side canyon below with a broken slope granting access to the mesa top. In the process, I was able to explore obscure ruins and view many other rarely visited sites from the perspective of the canyon rim. While I had expectations regarding my trip, I was able to be far more flexible at this point, and I found a great deal of beauty in the unexpected and in rearranging my plans. Our paths don't always lead where we would like. That doesn't mean, however, that life is not full of wonder and beauty, only that it will always be a complex thing we can adjust to.

This work invokes the idea of "sojourn" because understanding the nature of life as a journey is crucial to learning how to live correctly and navigate our way through this existence. We are at best travelers through this world, like one who journeys into the wilderness to discover what it has in store for him or her. We began by talking about how travels or sojourns into wild places can serve as an instructing metaphor that we need. These can provide us with perspective on lives that often fail and help us make sense after our expectations have been shattered. We are sojourners here. It is vital that we learn how to travel well. As Gabriel Marcel says, "Perhaps a stable order can only be established on earth if man always remains accurately conscious that his condition is that of a traveler."

The organizing concept of a sojourn is important in at least three ways. First, it brings to mind the image of one who is traveling away from home and detached from the comforts that tend to insulate us. Homes have become especially important in our culture as status symbols as well as places of refuge, not only from natural elements but often from a broken world as well. It is in the home that we surround ourselves with the comforts of heated or cooled air, plenty of unnecessary food, and the banal entertainments that serve as escapes from so much of life. In the current existential crises of many lives in the Western world, it is important to ask if this is really the best thing for us. A sojourn takes us away from these self-created and self-medicated environs so that reality can finally be confronted. In traveling, we come face-to-face with complexity, which in organisms as well as organizations is far more real than our self-constructed order or the chaos we often harbor within. If we travel well, we will recognize life as a weighty thing, and we may find release from the unbearable lightness of our isolated and lonely selves. It is in being separated from the comforts of home that we learn the value of fear and how we can actually use it to serve us. The wild places we learn to cultivate and travel in, even at the fearful expense of our groomed context, will be the source of the integration we are made for and long so desperately to find.

But the discovery is one out there in what the aborigines of Australia call a "walkabout." Whatever shuts us away from the waterfall and the tiger will eventually kill us.

Thoreau recognized, from his forays into the dark woods of Maine, that inexplicable wilderness carried him beyond himself, beyond all illusion of mastery, into an emptiness that left him stunned, vulnerable, and open to the unexpected. "We need the tonic of wilderness. ... At the same time that we are earnest to explore and learn all things, we require that all things be mysterious and unexplainable, that land and sea be infinitely wild, unsurveyed and unfathomed by us because unfathomable." (Lane, 1998)

Second, the idea of sojourn is invaluable for us because it teaches us what to do with liminal space—a life brought to the edge. Wild travels will inevitably bring us to the edge of our resources—physically, mentally, and hopefully spiritually. Away from the comfort and plentitude of the home, we can experience the end of our own resources and so be brought to the brink of the abyss, where an expansive new vista can open before us. I doubt that anyone can really get through life without facing some kind of liminality—the death of a loved one, the loss of a job, and empty nest, or the experience of who we have become at midlife. Will we be equipped to recognize such middle space when it comes? Will we have any idea of how to respond to being in "in-betweenness?" If we understand and practice traveling, we may.

> Much of the work of the biblical God and human destiny itself is to get people into liminal space and to keep them there long enough to learn something essential and genuinely new. It is the ultimate teachable space. In some sense, it is the only teachable space. So much so that many spiritual giants try to live their entire lives in permanent liminality. They try to live on the margins and on the periphery of the system so they will not get sucked in to its illusions and payoffs. They know it is the only position that ensures continued wisdom, even broader perspective, and even deeper compassion. Liminal space will almost always

feel counterintuitive, like a waste of time and not logical or rational at all. In fact, it must break your sense of practicality and function and move you into the nonfunctional world for a time. (Rohr, 2004)

This brings us to the third lesson of the sojourn—its countercultural, counterintuitive nature. To cultivate edge experiences and question the achievements and comforts of our lives' efforts flies in the face of what has been the goal for many of our forty or so years. The whole idea of being a sojourner and living as such brings to mind the reality that maybe we shouldn't be so "at home" in the culture we've created for ourselves. Perhaps there are values and habits and goals that are not as fulfilling as we thought they would be. Consumption, isolation, disengagement, and countless other cultural realities that we are steeped in likely do more harm to our souls than not. To understand life as a journey is to ask if a culture that engenders a false order, chaos, an unbearable lightness, and consummate safety is really the best thing for us. The litany of our cultural and personal crises should cause us to question whether or not this really is the home we want. In his collection of essays titled *Beyond the Wall*, Ed Abbey struggles with a particular journey into the desert and wonders why he would ever think of walking away from the comforts of home for a time. "Why do I do this? (My feet hurt) Why? Well, it's the need, I guess, for some sort of authentic experience. (My hip joint hurts) As opposed to the merely synthetic experience of books, movies, TV, regular urban living. (My neck hurts) To meet my God, my Maker, once again, face to face, beneath my feet, beyond my arms, above my head. (Will there be water at Cabeza Tank?)" (Abbey, 1984).

There is no doubt that in many ways, this whole concept of sojourning and learning life's lessons in wild places is counterintuitive and countercultural. Yet there have been too many men and women throughout history who have learned the invaluable lessons of how to thrive in their existence precisely through wild exposure to wild places, far too many for us to believe that this isn't a path to the fullness life was intended to be. Jesus delivered his most memorable sermon from the setting of an otherwise uninhabited place. During the first successful summit of an eight-thousand-meter peak in the Himalayas in 1950, Maurice Herzog wrote,

> We were in a savage and desolate cirque of mountains never before seen by men. No animal or plants could exist here. In the pure morning light this absence of all life, this utter destitution of nature, seemed only to intensify our own inner strength. How could we expect anyone else to understand the peculiar exhilaration that we drew from this barrenness when man's natural tendency is to be attracted to everything in nature that is lush and fruitful? (Herzog, 1952)

May we find a similar exhilaration and intensifying of inner strength as we learn to travel well.

> *And the end of all our exploring*
> *Will be to arrive where we started*
> *And know the place for the first time.*
> —T. S. Eliot

BIBLIOGRAPHY

Abbey, Ed. *Beyond the Wall: Essays from the Outside*. New York: Henry Holt and Company, 1984.

_____. *Desert Solitaire: A Season in the Wilderness*. New York, Ballantine Books, 1968.

Blehm, Eric. *The Last Season*. New York: Harper Perennial, 2007.

Bly, Robert. *Iron John: A Book About Men*. Cambridge, Mass.: Da Capo Press, 2004.

Burke, Edmund. *A Philosophical Enquiry into the Origin of our Ideas of the Sublime and Beautiful*. New York: Oxford University Press, 2008.

Camus, Albert. *The Plague*. New York: Vintage Books, 1972.

Childs, Craig. *House of Rain: Tracking a Vanished Civilization across the American Southwest.* New York: Little, Brown and Company, 2006.

_____. *The Secret Knowledge of Water: Discovering the Essence of the American Desert.* Seattle: Sasquatch Books, 2000.

Conrad, Joseph. *Heart of Darkness.* New York: Penguin Books, 1910.

_____. *Lord Jim.* New York: Harper and Row, 1899.

Coupland, Douglas. *Life After God.* New York: Pocket Books, 1994.

Crouch, Gregory. *Enduring Patagonia.* New York: Random House, 2002.

Diamond, Jared. *Collapse: How Societies Choose to Fail or Succeed.* New York: Penguin Books, 2005.

Gonzales, Laurence. *Deep Survival: Who Lives, Who Dies and Why.* New York: W. W. Norton and Co., 2003.

Griffiths, Tom. *Slicing the Silence: Voyaging to the Antarctic.* Cambridge: Harvard University Press, 2007.

Herzog, Maurice. *Annapurna: First Conquest of an 8,000 meter Peak.* New York: E. P. Dutton and Co., 1952.

Jensen, Mark. "Unbroken Chain." *Outside Magazine* (November 1, 2002).

Johnson, Steven. *Emergence: The Connected Lives of Ants, Brains, Cities and Software*. New York: Scribner, 2001.

Kauffman, Stuart: *At Home in the Universe: The Search for the Laws of Self-Organization and Complexity*. New York: Oxford University Press, 1995.

Kelsey, Joe. *Climbing and Hiking in the Wind River Mountains*, 2nd ed. Evergreen, Colo.: Chockstone Press, 1994.

Krakauer, Jon. *Into the Wild*. New York: Anchor Books, 1997.

Kundera, Milan. *The Unbearable Lightness of Being*. New York: Harper and Row, 1989.

Lane, Belden. *The Solace of Fierce Landscapes: Exploring Desert and Mountain Spirituality*. New York: Oxford University Press, 1998.

Lewis, C. S. *The Great Divorce*. New York: Harper Collins, 1946.

McClintock, James. *Nature's Kindred Spirits*. Madison, Wisc.: University of Wisconsin Press, 1994.

Moore, Robert and Douglas Gillette. *King, Warrior, Magician, Lover: Rediscovering the Archetypes of the Mature Masculine*. New York: Harper Collins, 1990.

Nash, Roderick. *Wilderness and the American Mind*, rev. ed. New Haven, Conn.: Yale University Press, 1967.

Pascal, Blaise. *Pensees*. Middlesex, England: Penguin Classics, 1970.

Rasmussen, Knud. *Across Arctic America: Narrative of the Fifth Thule Expedition.* Anchorage: University of Alaska Press, 1999.

Roach, Gerry. *Colorado's Fourteeners: From Hikes to Climbs,* 2nd ed. Golden, Colo.: Fulcrum Publishing, 1999.

Rohr, Richard. *Adam's Return: The Five Promises of Male Initiation.* New York: Crossroad Publishing, 2004.

_____. *The Wild Man's Journey: Reflections on Male Spirituality,* rev. ed. Cincinnati, Ohio: St. Anthony Messenger Press, 1996.

Rusho, W. L. ed. *Everett Ruess: A Vagabond for Beauty and Wilderness Journals.* Salt Lake City: Gibbs Smith, 2002.

Sheldrake, Philip. *Living Between Worlds: Place and Journey in Celtic Spirituality.* Cambridge: Cowley Publications, 1995.

Simpson, Joe. *This Game of Ghosts.* London: Vintage Books, 1994.

Stegner, Wallace. *All the Live Little Things.* New York: Penguin Books, 1967.

_____. *Angle of Repose.* New York: Fawcett Crest Books, 1971.

_____. *Marking the Sparrow's Fall: The Making of the American West.* New York: Henry Holt and Company, 1998.

_____. *The Sound of Mountain Water.* Lincoln: University of Nebraska Press, 1985.

Teale, Edwin, ed. *The Wilderness World of John Muir: A Selection from his Collected Works*. Boston: Houghton Mifflin, Co., 2001.

Tempest-Williams, Terry. *Red: Passion and Patience in the Desert*. New York: Pantheon Books, 2001.

Thoreau, Henry David. *Walden*. New York: Oxford University Press, 1999.

Van Dyke, John Charles. *The Desert: Further Studies in Natural Appearances*. New York: Charles Scribners Sons, 1901.

Waldrop, M. Mitchell. *Complexity: Emerging Science at the Edge of Order and Chaos*. New York: Touchstone, 1992.

Wolcott, Michael. "Bird Watching in the Desert." *Mountain Gazette*. July, 2012.

About the Author

After graduating from Denver Seminary with an M.Div Degree in Historical Theology in 1994, I moved with my family to plant churches in rural Southern Colorado. While we planted churches in a rural Western context and helped other planters begin additional new works nearby, we spent a great deal of our free time learning to enjoy the natural beauty of our surroundings. In 2003, as a result of successful endeavors in a difficult context, I was offered a position as the Director of Church Planting over a region of five western states. During the nearly three years as I worked out of a District Office in Omaha, Nebraska I found myself increasingly frustrated at the apparent disconnect between new church start-ups in an American context and a culture (particularly in the Western United States) which seemed to be detaching itself from the Christian faith. It was apparent that the church had bought into the consumer mentality which believed that the answers to any crisis were to be found in a greater influx of cash and resources. While larger churches continued to grow at the expense of smaller, local community churches, the overall picture of the Christian Church in America was in decline both numerically and in its apparent impact on behavior. This realization precipitated a more personal crisis for me. My family and I moved to Western Colorado where I began working as a roughneck on a drilling rig in 2006. Nearing my middle years, I became personally broken and frustrated with my own sense of wothlessness as my education and experiences seemed to have all been for naught. It was following a particularly dark year of my life and in the presence of a wise Christian counselor that I was finally able to piece together some sense of perspective on why I--and people like me--were apparently unable to find any anchorage in life. Along with my wife and three teenage children, I continue to live on the Western Slope of Colorado where I still roughneck and utilize every opportunity I can to escape to the wild places of the mountains and deserts where I find perspective. I spend a great deal of time backpacking, climbing and reading about wild places where I believe there remain some important sources of perspective too many of us in our consumptive, materialstic and mechanized culture have forgotten. My writing is an effort to provide an important interface between natural settings and our spirituality in order to help us face the eb and flow of life with some sort of balance and anchorage.

www.ingramcontent.com/pod-product-compliance
Lightning Source LLC
Chambersburg PA
CBHW022253290526
45785CB00015B/759